Memorial Services

HELD IN THE SENATE AND HOUSE OF REPRESENTATIVES
OF THE UNITED STATES, TOGETHER WITH
REMARKS PRESENTED IN EULOGY OF

Alben William Barkley

LATE A SENATOR FROM
KENTUCKY

Eighty-fourth Congress
Second Session

UNITED STATES
GOVERNMENT PRINTING OFFICE
WASHINGTON : 1956

PREPARED UNDER THE DIRECTION OF
THE JOINT COMMITTEE ON PRINTING

Contents

CONTENTS

CONTENTS

Biography

ALBEN WILLIAM BARKLEY was born near Lowes, Graves County, Ky., November 24, 1877; attended the public schools and was graduated from Marvin College, Clinton, Ky., in 1897; afterward attended Emory College, Oxford, Ga., and the University of Virginia Law School, Charlottesville, Va.; was admitted to the bar in 1901 and commenced practice in Paducah, McCracken County, Ky.; prosecuting attorney for McCracken County, Ky., 1905–1909; judge of McCracken County Court 1909–1913; chairman of the Democratic State Conventions in 1919 and 1924; delegate to all Democratic National Conventions from 1920 to 1940, inclusive, serving as temporary chairman in 1932 and 1936 and as permanent chairman in 1940; elected as a Democrat to the Sixty-third and to the six succeeding Congresses (March 4, 1913–March 3, 1927); did not seek renomination in 1926, having become a candidate for United States Senator; elected to the United States Senate in 1926; reelected in 1932, 1938, and again in 1944, and served from March 4, 1927, until his resignation on January 19, 1949; served as Democratic majority leader of the Senate 1937–1947 and as Democratic minority leader of the Senate in 1947 and 1948; elected Vice President of the United States on the Democratic ticket with President Harry S. Truman in 1948, and was inaugurated January 20, 1949, for the term ending January 20, 1953; again elected to the United States Senate and served from January 3, 1955, until his death in Lexington, Va., April 30, 1956; interment in Mount Kenton Cemetery, on Lone Oak Road, near Paducah, Ky.

Memorial Services
for
Alben William Barkley

Eighty-fourth Congress
Second Session

Proceedings in the Senate

Mr. HAYDEN. Mr. President, in behalf of the Senator from Kentucky [Mr. Clements], who is absent from the Senate, attending the funeral of the late Senator BARKLEY, in Paducah, Ky., I submit a resolution, and ask for its present consideration. It is the purpose that at a later time a day will be set aside upon which appropriate eulogies may be pronounced by the colleagues of the late Senator in the Senate, and at this time I merely ask for action on the resolution.

The PRESIDENT pro tempore. The resolution will be read.

The legislative clerk read as follows:

Resolved, That the Senate has heard with profound sorrow and deep regret the announcement of the death of Hon. ALBEN W. BARKLEY, late a Senator from the State of Kentucky and a former Vice President of the United States.

Resolved, That a committee be appointed by the President of the Senate, who shall be a member of the committee, to attend the funeral of the deceased Senator at Paducah, Ky.

Resolved, That the Secretary communicate these resolutions to the House of Representatives and transmit a copy thereof to the family of the deceased.

The PRESIDENT pro tempore. Is there objection to the request of the Senator from Arizona?

There being no objection, the resolution (S. Res. 258) was considered by unanimous consent, and unanimously agreed to.

The PRESIDENT pro tempore. Pursuant to the second resolving clause, the Chair appoints, as the committee to attend the funeral of the late Senator, in addition to the Vice President, the Senator from Nevada [Mr. Bible], the Senator from Indiana [Mr. Capehart], the Senator from Kentucky [Mr. Clements], the Senator from Idaho [Mr.

Dworshak], the senior Senator from Mississippi [Mr. East-land], the Senator from North Carolina [Mr. Ervin], the Senator from Delaware [Mr. Frear], the Senator from Arkansas [Mr. Fulbright], the Senator from Georgia [Mr. George], the junior Senator from Tennessee [Mr. Gore], the Senator from Arizona [Mr. Hayden], the senior Senator from Alabama [Mr. Hill], the Senator from Minnesota [Mr. Humphrey], the Senator from Texas [Mr. Johnson], the senior Senator from South Carolina [Mr. Johnston], the senior Senator from Tennessee [Mr. Kefauver], the Senator from Oklahoma [Mr. Kerr], the junior Senator from West Virginia [Mr. Laird], the Senator from Michigan [Mr. Mc-Namara], the Senator from Oregon [Mr. Morse], the senior Senator from West Virginia [Mr. Neely], the Senator from Wyoming [Mr. O'Mahoney], the Senator from Rhode Island [Mr. Pastore], the Senator from Connecticut [Mr. Purtell], the Senator from Kansas [Mr. Schoeppel], the junior Senator from Alabama [Mr. Sparkman], the junior Senator from Mississippi [Mr. Stennis], the Senator from Missouri [Mr. Symington], and the junior Senator from South Carolina [Mr. Wofford].

Mr. HAYDEN. Mr. President, I move that, as a further mark of respect to the memory of the deceased, the Senate stand in adjournment until Monday next at 12 o'clock noon.

The motion was unanimously agreed to; and (at 12 o'clock and 4 minutes p. m.) the Senate adjourned until Monday, May 7, 1956, at 12 o'clock meridian.

MONDAY, *May 7, 1956.*

The Chaplain, Rev. Frederick Brown Harris, D. D., offered the following prayer:

Our Father, God, as we turn to Thee, who knowest the sadness which grips our spirits, we mourn the passing from this mortal stage of one who was adored and trusted by a vast host of his fellow countrymen.

[12]

Hundreds saw him die—millions saw him live. The Nation which he loved and served saw him live across self-giving decades; for he lived and wrought with ardent passion for the preservation undimmed of the spiritual verities upon which the Republic was founded by God-fearing men.

We remember gratefully today—now that an honored seat in this Chamber is vacant—that freedom's holy light, which is America, was his creed, and that he dedicated every power of his being for its defense. Proudly he walked around freedom's ramparts which he helped to watch, perceiving with elert eyes the dire dangers which threatened her very survival in these days of her most crucial test.

We thank Thee that the burning words of his impassioned voice, as he pleaded for the faith that burned like fire in his bones within these hallowed walls and up and down the land, will forever be a part of the heritage of this body as he joins the cloud of witnesses whose membership depends not on any election but upon the selection by a nation which gladly acknowledges his eminence, as he did justly, loved mercy, and walked humbly with his God.

So teach us to number our remaining days that we may apply our hearts unto wisdom, and at last, like him, to enter into the inheritance of the saints in light: In the name of the Master he acknowledged the Lord of all. Amen.

Mr. CLEMENTS. Mr. President, it is my present intention to comment on the passing of our late, beloved colleague, Senator ALBEN W. BARKLEY. At an early time in the future, agreeable to the families of both the late Senator BARKLEY and the late Senator HARLEY M. KILGORE, a suitable day for memorial tributes to them will be set aside.

What I say now is entirely personal, generated and impelled by the poignant sense of personal loss I have experienced at the death of Senator BARKLEY.

In the past few days we have, as mourners, walked near the valley of the shadow.

The shadows of that valley are long and extend even to this Chamber where today our lives are touched with its darkness.

And though the flag over the Capitol of the United States is again at full mast, there has been no like uplifting of our hearts, no lessening of the hurt we feel at the passing of ALBEN BARKLEY, a man we loved, a man we respected, a man we needed.

The last few days have but sharpened the pain and magnified the loss to those who were his colleagues, to those who were his family, to all those—and they must be counted in the millions—who loved him.

We here knew him best, for it was here—in this Chamber he loved and served so well—that he labored for his State, his Nation, and his people.

It is at a time like this that the man who would speak his thoughts discovers, once again, the terrible thinness of words.

At a time like this a man sees once again, that vast no-man's land that lies between thought and expression, between emotion and articulation.

At a time like this, a man discovers that though his heart be eloquent, his words are paltry.

Men have said of ALBEN BARKLEY that he was like an oak. And surely he was.

When I think of an oak, I think of how it grows, and how with each year, another ring is added beneath the bark. ALBEN BARKLEY was an oak, yes, and he had 51 golden rings, to mark the 51 years of his service to his State and Nation.

Last year was his golden anniversary of service.

He served his Nation as few men have served it, and we here today would do well, in our hearts, were we to resolve to try to serve as he did.

In this time of grief we, in our human, mortal way, seek thoughts that will give us some comfort, thoughts that will soften the terrible blow, that will help us adjust our hearts and minds to the incomprehensible truth that ALBEN BARKLEY is gone.

I find some comfort in the thought that the last sound ALBEN BARKLEY heard was the sound of the American people applauding. The young Americans attending a student political convention in Lexington, Va., had just applauded his words when he fell. The sound of their applause still hung in the air, and I like to think that the applause of the American people, which he deserved so well, was the sound that ALBEN BARKLEY carried with him into eternity.

I also find some comfort when I realize that Senator BARKLEY lived each day of his life to the full, lived each day as though it were his last. His life, every day of his 78 years, was such a good one that it could be ended suddenly, without fear that the last thought or the last action would not be pleasing to the Almighty Father.

So it was that when he was called home by the loving Father, ALBEN BARKLEY was ready, and his last words were as fine as a good man can speak—words that have been on the lips of many people throughout the world:

I would rather be a servant in the house of the Lord than sit in the seat of the mighty.

We all know that he served in the house of the Lord, and that he served well.

We here also know, that he served in the house of democracy. And we know that he served well. Few men, in all of mankind's long struggle for freedom, for democracy, have served the house of democracy so well.

Today, I am profoundly aware that ALBEN BARKLEY was a great man, a truly great man. Today, I am also profoundly aware that he will continue to serve us as a source of inspiration.

Since 1905, ALBEN BARKLEY, a great Kentuckian, a great American, helped America achieve her full maturity as a nation.

As Representative in Congress, Senator, Vice President, and statesman he helped clear the frontiers of an adult America—frontiers dark with economic, social, and humanitarian problems. He was one of those who made our recent past a golden age in American development. Between 1937 and 1947, he was the majority leader of this great body, and guided into being much of the great legislation of that historic decade.

Following the war his great, tireless voice was raised in a call for responsibility and America met her responsibility as a great world power.

ALBEN BARKLEY was a man known by many names. To the Nation he was the beloved "Veep." To the Democratic Party he was "Mr. Democrat." To the Commonwealth of Kentucky, he was the "Kentuckian." To us, he was a "Senator's Senator."

America will remember ALBEN BARKLEY.

We will remember him.

We will remember him here in this Chamber, and though ALBEN BARKLEY'S great voice is stilled, the memory of his words, of his deeds, and of his actions for God, country, and State, will speak to us as long as there is a United States of America, as long as there is a Senate of the United States, as long as there is an American people.

Mr. President, I request unanimous consent to have printed in the body of the Record the beautiful prayer offered by the Senate Chaplain, Rev. Frederick Brown Harris, D. D., at the funeral services of our beloved friend and distinguished colleague, the Honorable ALBEN W. BARKLEY, at the Foundry Methodist Church, Wednesday, May 2, 1956.

There being no objection, the prayer was ordered to be printed in the Record, as follows:

Let us now praise famous men and our fathers that begat us, leaders of the people, by their counsels honored in their generation and the glory of their time; that have left a name behind them that their praises might be reported. Their bodies are buried in peace, but their names liveth for evermore.

ALBEN WILLIAM BARKLEY

Let us lift our hearts in prayer:

O Thou Master of all good workmen: We come to Thy sanctuary this hour with a sense of poignant loss, vividly conscious of an empty place against the sky—at which our surprised eyes are staring, stunned, bewildered, and strangely moved. We sit together in the sadness of farewell as we mourn the sudden passing from our sight and side of one of the greatest of our national leaders— for there is a prince and a great man fallen. One of the Republic's best-loved sons—Thy servant across toiling years in all great and good cause—ALBEN W. BARKLEY.

From our partial, finite point of view his State and the Nation, which he served with such unstinted devotion, are vastly poorer because his eloquent, passionate voice will be heard no more in its councils, on its platforms, and in its national forums. For us, there is an altered world since but a few hours ago he "went down in full armour", with unabated powers, having lived his strenuous years up to the hilt. He so numbered his days, applying his heart unto wisdom, because to him the whole earth was the House of the Lord, as echoed by the last phrase which fell from his lips.

And now we come in gratitude to think tenderly of one who occupied high office, and yet never stooped to low designs; who was greatly honored by his countrymen, but who ever put principle above pedestal; who was a partisan, with deep convictions, yet without a blind spot that cannot see the integrity of an opponent's position.

We exalt the memory this hour of one who walked with kings nor lost the common touch, who could remain silent under unjust attack—as he often did—exemplifying that "he who keepeth his own spirit is greater than he who taketh a city."

We think of one who with unbowed head and unembittered heart met life's losses, and who found constant fun in living, and who reveled in laughter; who loved folks more than fortunate, and who was valiant as a knight of old, in righting wrongs and enthroning justice; and who counted it as a part of his religion to help see that his country was well governed.

While we mourn that we shall see his face no more, solemnize us by the uncertainty of our own working day. May we lengthen our brief span by intensity of living, filling swift hours with mighty deeds. If there is any kindness we can show, may we not neglect nor defer it—seeing that we pass this way but once.

And thus, at last, O Lord of the living and of the living dead, bring us all to the Homeland of Thine eternal love. We ask it through the riches of grace in Christ Jesus our Lord. Amen.

Mr. CLEMENTS. Mr. President, I have a record of the services at the Broadway Methodist Church at Paducah, Ky., last Thursday. They were conducted by the Reverend William S. Evans, pastor of the church. I ask unanimous consent that the text of the services be printed in the Record.

There being no objection, the text was ordered to be printed in the Record, as follows:

Dr. EVANS. I shall read the 23d Psalm:

"The Lord is my shepherd; I shall not want.

"He maketh me to lie down in green pastures; He leadeth me beside the still waters.

"He restoreth my soul: He leadeth me in the paths of righteousness for His name's sake.

"Yea, though I walk through the valley of the shadow of death, I will fear no evil: for Thou art with me; Thy rod and Thy staff they comfort me.

"Thou preparest a table before me in the presence of mine enemies: Thou anointest my head with oil; my cup runneth over.

"Surely goodness and mercy shall follow me all the days of my life: and I will dwell in the house of the Lord forever."

I now read John 14: 1-4:

"Let not your heart be troubled: ye believe in God, believe also in me.

"In my Father's house are many mansions: if it were not so, I would have told you.

"And if I go and prepare a place for you, I will come again, and receive you unto myself; that where I am, there ye may be also.

"And whither I go ye know, and the way ye know."

It would be presumptuous on my part to undertake to eulogize such a person as the Honorable ALBEN W. BARKLEY. He needs no eulogy. His life has been one long testimony of his faith and convictions. However, I would not be faithful to the many multiplied thousands of friends who are here in this sanctuary and who are at this moment turning their thoughts and minds toward this service, did I not give some word of appreciation. There was something inherent in his life that make all want to do him honor. It stirs the hearts of all of us to think of one who came from humble surroundings and who rose through hard work and persistent zeal to stand as one of the most honored men in our

Nation. He was one who won and kept the confidence of men of all walks of life, and who received expressions of that confidence as he was placed in many places of responsibility and leadership.

When news of his passing reached me at the general conference of our church in Minneapolis, Minn., I asked the privilege of that world gathering that we might stand in a moment of silent tribute to the life of this great man.

Certainly a part of the life story of Mr. BARKLEY would be found in the character of his parents. But, also, much resided within his own life. He had a vision of something big. He had a determination to pay the price to achieve greatness. He had a willingness to follow on. To my way of thinking, one of the secrets of success of life is expressed in the words of Kipling, who, as he undertook to give the measurements of man, said,

> "If you can walk with kings
> Nor lose the common touch."

Mr. BARKLEY certainly had that quality in his life. Across his beloved State and throughout the Nation and the world men have loved him, respected his integrity, followed his counsel, and have been enriched by his personality.

Many honors came to him, but no honor was greater than the sincere appreciation and high esteem in which he is held by those that knew him best. Today, as he comes back to rest in the soil of his beloved State, many, many people will rise up to call him blessed and thank God for having been privileged to be his friend.

In this service we would lift up to you some words that might strengthen our lives for the facing of this hour and the living of these days. One of the ancient men of God expressed a conviction that held him, and which I think will hold us. He said, "The Eeternal God is thy refuge, and underneath are the everlasting arms."

As we pass through shadows and carry our loads of grief, may we be strengthened by knowing that the Eeternal God is good. As he was revealed in Christ, His sympathy, love, and compassion reached out to those in sorrow. And in our times of sorrow and suffering we can be comforted by the fact that God cares. God cares because He loves us. In one of their Psalms, the ancient people of Zion sang, "I had fainted unless I had believed to see the goodness of the Lord in the land of the living." You can't read the great 23d Psalm without realizing that God is good. He is there pictured as the Great Shepherd who, though we "Walk through the valley of the shadow of death," He will be with us. Whittier said:

> "Yet, in the maddening maze of things
> And tossed by storm and flood,
> To one fixed trust my spirit clings;
> I know that God is good."

"The Eternal God is thy refuge, and underneath are the everlasting arms." (Deuteronomy 33: 27.)

God is also great. His arms have never failed. The refuge that is offered in Him covers our needs. "His grace is sufficient." Those who have trusted Him, those who have talked with Him, those who have tested Him have found that His promises are true and that His word never fails. So, as we walk and as we live we can lean our lives upon God, who is great.

"As the marsh hen builds on the watery sod
    I will build me a nest on the greatness of God;
I will fly in the greatness of God as the marsh hen flies,
    In the freedom that fills all the space 'twixt the earth and
        the skies.
By so many roots as the marsh grass sends into the sod,
    I will heartily lay me a hold on the greatness of God."

When you begin to read your Bible, you find that "In the beginning, God," and when you read the description of the last Hallelujah Chorus, you find that God is from everlasting to everlasting. He truly has been "Our dwelling place in all generations." The Eternal God that is our refuge does not change with the changing seasons. He is not ruled by the rulers of darkness. And he is not defeated by the experience of death. When you begin to think of the things that will live and last, you immediately begin to realize that these are characteristics of God: Beauty, purity of heart, nobleness of character—they never die. Truth may be ignored, assailed, crushed to earth, trampled upon, yet truth lives. Beauty also lives. Tertullian once said, "If I give you a rose, you won't doubt God any more." Beauty is of God. We are told that knowledge will pass away, but love will abide. In our time of greatest need, the love of the Eternal is most wonderfully kind.

I am simply saying that, as we rest our lives in the Eternal God, we have laid hold upon something that is eternal. In Him we live, move, and have our being. In Him we live forever. I am reminded of the last words that fell from the lips of Mr. BARKLEY:

"I would rather be a servant in the House of the Lord than sit in the seat of the mighty."

As we give our lives in service to the good and noble things, we find a life for ourselves that lives. And in Christ we can have the assurance of a life that never dies. It was said of one of the great characters in the Old Testament: "David, after he had served his own generation, by the will of God, fell asleep and was laid unto his fathers." In this faith we, too, may live.

Mr. CLEMENTS. Mr. President, I ask unanimous consent to have printed in the Record a significant telegram which was forwarded to our Senate Chaplain, Rev. Frederick Brown Harris, by Mr. W. P. Kennedy, president of the Brotherhood of Railroad Trainmen, as an expression of genuine regret over the great loss which has been suffered in the passing of our beloved colleague and courageous statesman, the Honorable ALBEN W. BARKLEY.

There being no objection, the telegram was ordered to be printed in the Record, as follows:

CLEVELAND, OHIO, *May 1, 1956.*

Rev. FREDERICK BROWN HARRIS,
   The Westchester, Washington, D. C.:
Members of the Brotherhood of Railroad Trainmen throughout the land are deeply grieved over the untimely loss of Senator BARKLEY. He was our friend. He fought for our rights when we had few friends. In all public offices held he was always ready, anxious, and willing to serve his fellow men. The millions who love and cherish decency, dignity, and honesty in government will join in mourning the loss of this great American, our beloved Senator BARKLEY.

W. P. KENNEDY, *President.*

Mr. CLEMENTS. Mr. President, many fine editorials have been written about the life of ALBEN BARKLEY, and many of them will be placed in the Record by other Members of the Senate. At this time I ask unanimous consent to have printed in the Record editorials published in the Lexington Herald, the Owensboro Messenger and Inquirer, and the Louisville Courier-Journal.

There being no objection, the editorials were ordered to be printed in the Record as follows:

[From the Lexington (Ky.) Herald of May 1, 1956]

A VOICE THAT IS STILLED

Death came to ALBEN W. BARKLEY as he invited it, as a Member of the United States Senate which he loved and in which he had long served and over which he presided, and during a speech to a convention of young Democrats. Thus falls the elder statesman speaking to the younger generation, preaching the gospel of democracy.

Only a few days ago, at the observance of the Woodrow Wilson centennial in Washington, he had poured out the philosophy of politics of which he was the most gifted exponent. He and Speaker of the House Sam Rayburn had entered the House of Representatives the same day, the year Woodrow Wilson became President of the United States.

For 44 years in Washington and for more than 50 years in Kentucky he had answered the call to public service, holding office longer than any man in the history of the commonwealth, including Henry Clay.

Appraisal and analysis of his record can wait a day while all Kentuckians, with partisanship or factionalism forgotten, mourn the passing of a statesman upon whose long years of service there was no stain or corruption, who gave all he had in the public interest. The last of the old-fashioned orators, the master of the story-tellers, the beloved Veep, the former president of the American delegation to the Inter-Parliamentary Union, one of the first advocates of the United Nations, the greatest of all convention keynoters, now sleeps with his fathers. He might have gained a Vice Presidential nomination that would have led to the Presidency, had not his conviction forced him to differ over a tax measure with a President to whom he was devoted. He did in 1948 stir from its lethargy a party that had about succumbed to defeatism, and a notable Democratic triumph resulted. He knew all the plaudits of victory, yet suffered in 1952 a defeat that might have stopped a less determined soul. But he loved people and they called him back to the Senate, which numbers him among the greatest who ever served within its Chamber.

He was and will ever be, for all time to come, Kentucky's favorite son.

ALBEN WILLIAM BARKLEY

[From the Lexington (Ky.) Herald of May 2, 1956]

MR. BARKLEY'S BELIEFS

As Kentucky officially observes a period of mourning in the memory of former Vice President ALBEN W. BARKLEY, the Nation is grieved over the death of a beloved figure. His services on the national scene extended over a period of nearly half a century. Those things for which Mr. BARKLEY so clearly stood should not be overlooked in paying homage, either to the personality whose magnetism charmed the American people from coast to coast, or to the public career which is without parallel in Kentucky's history.

The close of his career crowned a lifetime of what he so often had called "preaching the gospel of democracy." He was stricken while appearing as a keynoter, the role he had filled so often in Democratic national conventions, before a mock convention of young voters at Washington and Lee University. It is easy to imagine the beauties of the day for he had been at the annual party given at the home of Senator Harry F. Byrd near Winchester, Va., to Members of Congress. From the porch where guests are served, no doubt he looked upon the familiar scene at the head of the Shenandoah Valley where the famed Byrd apple orchard was in bloom, before going to the campus of Washington and Lee University whose classic buildings patterned after Arlington and Monticello remind all of the priceless heritage of the Republic.

There could be no more thrilling words than those uttered:

"I would rather be a servant in the house of the Lord than to sit in the seats of the mighty."

And while in the Senate of the United States Mr. BARKLEY had a forum which gave to him the unexcelled opportunity to use the gift of his rare knowledge gained by long observation, he spent much of his time going out to explain, as he viewed them, the issues that face this country and the world. Time and time again he came to Kentucky to the annual Jefferson-Jackson Day dinners staged by the Democratic Party but explained that with him the fund-raising objective was not paramount, that as long as his body held breath he wished to repeat the things he had seen and that he knew about government, legislation, and national policies. Frequently he said, as he did after withdrawing as a candidate

[23]

for the Democratic nomination for the Presidency in the national convention at Chicago in 1952:

"We are not beginning a crusade. We are continuing a crusade."

His great speech delivered April 21 in the National Guard Armory in Washington in connection with the Woodrow Wilson centennial carried out this theme. He had entered his service in the House of Representatives in 1913, the year Woodrow Wilson became President of the United States. The Federal Reserve System, the Clayton antitrust enactments, the curbing and reduction of child labor, the inauguration of the farm-credit system, civil-service reform, and many other advanced strides were steps in which he had a hand.

Yet it was the fact that the first great effort since the Congress in Vienna in 1815 to organize the world for peace came from Woodrow Wilson's heart and brain that primarily characterized that administration, as Mr. BARKLEY pictured it from his vivid and retentive memory.

One of the greatest and most effective political speeches ever delivered in the history of this country was Mr. BARKLEY's address to the Democratic National Convention in 1948. This convention later nominated him for the Vice Presidency. Although Mr. Truman in his recent book refers to his own appearance, it was the speech that Senator BARKLEY delivered that electrified and awakened that convention from a pall of defeatism to a victory march. In these columns it frequently has been said that this single speech more than any other factor led to the election of Truman and Barkley in 1948. The "cross of gold" speech of William Jennings Bryan is long remembered, but it led the party only to defeat. Mr. BARKLEY gained for his party 4 years of responsibility during which the United Nations was launched, as Mr. BARKLEY said, "upon the tossing waters of the international sea," and the Marshall plan served as a prelude to the attempt to wage peace in the world.

It was the record that had been made, not only by the Democratic Party but by the Congress of the United States which enacted the legislation and through bipartisan support in drafting the charter of the United Nations, that he upheld. It was because Congress, after long hearings and committee action and deliberation, had adopted a tax bill which President Roosevelt vetoed that he split with the President and offered to resign as floor leader, thus eliminating himself as a Vice Presidential prospect in 1944.

This record he was willing and ready to defend. That was the theme of his masterful presentation in Philadelphia, for he asked why the members of his party were apologizing, defending, and dodging rather than affirming, proclaiming, and championing the steps that they had taken to take the farmer out of the ditch of despondency, to see that every American had a decent home and to conserve the soil and to undertake to bring about a life of security and peace.

Step by step, law by law, amendment by amendment, Mr. BARK-LEY knew the details of the legislation enacted to establish foreign policy and domestic progress. He never lost faith in the people or their ability to think straight and act in the best interests of the country when the truth was fully presented to them. He risked his life unsparingly, and finally gave it in that cause.

[From the Owensboro (Ky.) Messenger and Inquirer of May 1, 1956]
DEATH OF "VEEP" COMES AS GRIEVOUS SHOCK

We were indeed shocked and grieved to learn yesterday of the loss of our friend ALBEN W. BARKLEY. Despite his 78 years we still considered the "Veep" a young man with many years of public service yet before him.

Our most recent contact with the famous Kentucky gentleman was during the past senatorial race when he came to Owensboro to speak on his own behalf. This was just 2 years ago when he made his race against another great Kentuckian, representing the opposing party, John Sherman Cooper.

We were truly convinced that the name of "Iron Man" given to him in his race for the Senate in 1926 held as true 2 years ago as it held in that bygone race. The "Veep" in his most recent race was the war horse, the great wit and entertainer, the fast thinker he must have been 30 years ago.

But our observations of this Democrat were even more meaningful when one considers some of the rocky roads he had traveled during his political career, especially those thorny incidents which occurred late in his life.

BARKLEY was on two occasons within the grasp of the Presidency. If it had not been for his independence as speaker in the Senate during the Roosevelt administration he might have been President. It was his rebuff of President Roosevelt which kept him out as the Vice Presidential candidate on the ticket with FDR. He had criticized the chief for what he considered interference with the independence of Congress. As a result Truman got the call and filled out the late President's term.

The Presidency was again within the grasp of the Iron Man when he went to Chicago in 1952. The day before the convention opened, the head of the Kentucky delegation, Gov. Lawrence Wetherby, stated that the greatest danger to BARKLEY was the strength the Vice President had amassed just prior to the convention. The danger proved to be real and devastating. It brought out the mean and crucifying words "too old" to run. The coup executed by some labor leaders was a final blow to his candidacy. BARKLEY in his autobiography attributed his withdrawal at the Chicago convention to a selfish faction within the party which cut him out. In our opinion this was only a part of the story.

He did not know how close he came to the Presidency until Harry Truman's memoirs were published, in which the former President said that if BARKLEY had not withdrawn as a candidate for the Democratic nomination in Chicago in 1952, after it was made to appear to some that labor would not support him because of his age, he would have been nominated.

This newspaper believed in 1952 that it was true that at the convention in Chicago Harry S. Truman had decided to throw his great and decisive support to BARKLEY. We did not know it was true until Truman's memoirs appeared with the emphatic statement that if BARKLEY had not withdrawn—which he did at the instigation of poorly informed advisers—he would have won the nomination.

We felt that the difference between votes for Stevenson and the votes BARKLEY would have received, in our humble opinion, would have meant the difference between success and failure for the Democrats in 1952.

Senator BARKLEY aspired to the Presidency as possibly no other man. He felt his experience in government particularly suited him for that high position, and he wanted to offer himself to the people so that he could better serve them. Even though he sought the position, he never felt that the people owed him their allegiance because of what he had done for them, and he had done much.

Coming from a predominately agricultural State, he had done much for the farmer, but he had also done much for industry, and had never forgotten that this segment of the American economy was equally important. During the NRA days, which business fought violently, the Senator from Kentucky went to bat for local industry and averted troubles which could have been disastrous to Owensboro and other parts of the State. His experiences went throughout the scope of government.

ALBEN WILLIAM BARKLEY

When Senator BARKLEY became Vice President during the second Truman administration, his experience enabled him to fulfill a function of government never tried by his vice presidential predecessors. He not only served as the President of the Senate, but really as an assistant President. He advised Truman and helped in party affairs. His participation in Truman's campaign during the former President's campaign against Dewey was, in our opinion, the clincher in the Nation's greatest political upset.

We believe his experiences would have embittered other men to the point that their services to the people would have been drastically limited.

When we saw BARKLEY here 2 years ago he was humble, unscarred by disappointment, and anxious to serve if the people wanted him. He had adopted his own formula for a long and productive life, that of working a full day, honesty and maintaining a clear conscience.

One of his parting words to us, and significant of his life was: "I would rather be a servant in the house of the Lord than sit in the seat of the mighty."

This we know to be true for we knew the man who said them.

We shared his disappointment in not realizing his ambition to become President. Now we share with his friends the loss to our State and our Nation of one of its greatest and most faithful leaders.

[From the Louisville Courier-Journal of May 2, 1956]

ALBEN BARKLEY GAVE MORE THAN LOYALTY TO PARTY

ALBEN W. BARKLEY was a man of the people. His basic political conviction was that Government ought to serve them. It was his conception that the Democratic Party was better able to serve their needs, and on this was set the solid rock of his party loyalty.

During his career in politics, however, Mr. BARKLEY gave his party more than loyalty. He gave it the full measure of his own concern for people, a concern unbound either by acceptance or rejection of the catch phrases of political dogma. He saw no creeping socialism in the Tennessee Valley Authority; to him it was good because it helped a region's people. Although he could throw political stilettos with the best, a man was not an economic royalist to him merely because he was rich. What he did oppose was exploitation of the people.

ALBEN BARKLEY'S two political idols were Abraham Lincoln and Woodrow Wilson. To him the former embodied the American legend and the latter the intellectual spirit of the Democratic Party. It may fairly be said that Mr. BARKLEY himself came to embody the American legend, and that he, too, was a repository of the Democratic spirit. It is ironic that he missed the Presidency once because in 1944 Franklin Roosevelt passed him over for Harry Truman as a vice presidential nominee, and that in 1952 he missed the presidential nomination because his old friends, the labor leaders, though him too old at 74. These must surely have been bitter disappointments to him, but he was not a man given to self pity. After his extraordinarily long service in Congress, and after his endearing role as the Veep, he went back to the upper house in 1954, as Kentucky's junior Senator with all the zest and relish that were his stock in trade.

It was in true character that this remarkable man would not let himself run down. To the very end he showed the self-discipline and apparently unbounded energy that had carved his special niche in American political lore. A master storyteller, an elder statesman, a political craftsman and the possessor of a quick and cheerful wit, Mr. BARKLEY was enjoying himself keynoting the mock Democratic convention at Washington and Lee University. There always awakened a sort of affinity between ALBEN BARKLEY and his audiences. He prided himself on the fact that he didn't preach sermonettes. Indeed his sonorous voice was more at home in the old-style open-air political rally than in the modulated, closely timed confines of modern sound transmission. But loud or soft, long or brief, ALBEN BARKLEY's speeches always semed to be spoken directly to each of his listeners. It may have been simply because he so truly liked people that they couldn't help liking him back.

At any rate, when he told the students at Lexington, Va., "I'd rather be a servant in the house of the Lord than sit in the seat of the mighty," and collapsed and died, it surely must have been as he would have had it. We, his fellow Kentuckians, are saddened deeply, but we are as proud of ALBEN BARKLEY as we can be.

Mr. CLEMENTS. Mr. President on Tuesday evening, after the passing of my distinguished colleague, a number of Members of the Senate and Members of the House made statements for a radio program conducted by one of the great radio stations of the country. I have a transcription of that program, and I ask unanimous consent that it may be printed in the body of the Record at this point.

There being no objection, the transcription was ordered to be printed in the Record, as follows:

Senator CLEMENTS. The Father of us all has called home one of His favorite sons. He was, as all of you know, called suddenly and unexpectedly. And because ALBEN BARKLEY was throughout his life a devoted son to the Almighty Father he answered the call of the Father quickly and without protest. For his family, his Nation, his State, this is a time of grief. In this time of grief we, in our human mortal way, seek thoughts that will give us some comfort—thoughts that will soften this terrible blow, that will help us adjust our hearts and minds to the incomprehensible truth that ALBEN BARKLEY—a man we love—is gone. I find some comfort in the thought that the last sound ALBEN BARKLEY heard was the sound of the American people applauding. The young Americans attending a student political convention in Lexington, Va., had just applauded his words when he fell. The sound of their applause still hung in the air and I like to think that the applause of the American people which he deserved so well was the sound that Senator ALBEN BARKLEY carried with him into eternity. I also find some comfort when I realize that Senator BARKLEY lived each day of his life to the full. Lived each day as thought it were his last. His life—every day of his 78 years and more—was such a good one that it could be ended suddenly, without fear that the last thought or the last action would not be pleasing to the Almighty Father. So it was that when he was called, ALBEN BARKLEY was ready. And his last words were as fine as a good man can speak. "I would rather be a servant in the House of the Lord than sit in the seat of the Mighty." We all know that he served in the House of the Lord and served well. We all know, too, that he served in what could be called under these tragic circumstances the house of democracy. And few men in all of mankind's long struggle for freedom for democracy have served that house—the house of democracy—so well. Today, I am profoundly aware that ALBEN BARKLEY was a great man, a truly great man. He served his country for a half a century. He serves us all today, as he did yesterday, as a source of inspiration. We who survive can be eternally grateful that we knew ALBEN BARKLEY for knowing him was to know a man who possessed the heart, the mind, the courage, the energy, and, yes, the conscience of greatness. I knew him for more than 30 years in an intimate and personal way. I knew him as only those in public life can know what a monumental contribution he made to the government of his State of Kentucky and to the Government of the United States.

His career is without parallel. He was born in a log cabin on a farm in Graves County in Kentucky on November 24, 1877.

In the years that followed, he rose to the heights, but the climb was a long and tiring one. He put himself through school sweeping floors. He practiced law and in 1904 he made his first political speech. The next year riding a horse to his first campaign victory he was elected prosecuting attorney of McCracken County. He later served the same county as its county judge. He went on to the House of Representatives, being elected in the year of 1912 from the First District of Kentucky. He was sworn in on the day that Woodrow Wilson took the oath of office of President of the United States, and there was destiny in that fact for throughout his long career as Congressman, as Senator, as Vice President the principles of Woodrow Wilson were Senator BARKLEY's guiding star. ALBEN BARKLEY believed in fundamental democracy. His political philosophy, as he expressed it to me on many occasions, was this: "What was good for the greatest number of people was best for the whole of the people." I was, throughout the 30 years I knew him, his supporter, his friend, his admirer. Today those who knew and loved ALBEN BARKLEY are telling and retelling some of his fine stories that have made him a living legend as a public speaker. Today I recall those stories, too. But something else, too. Something even more enduring. The great pieces of legislation that went through the Senate during the period of 1937–47 when ALBEN BARKLEY was the majority leader of the United States Senate. America will remember ALBEN BARKLEY for his sponsorship of and leadership in putting through much of the important and beneficial legislation of the 1930's, for his vision and leadership in such vital decisions as lend-lease, and ratification of the United Nations Charter. America will remember his great voice raised in great causes. The Senate will remember him as a Senator's Senator. The people will remember him as their beloved Veep; his family as a noble, warm, and loved man. ALBEN BARKLEY's voice is still but the memory of his words, of his deeds, and of his actions for God, country, and State will go on as long as there is an America and an American people. My friends, at this time I want to present one who learned of these eulogies for our distinguished friend who is gone, when he was away from the Capitol. He will be heard by telephone and I have reference to one who came to the House about the time Senator BARKLEY did, served with Senator BARKLEY for 14 years in the House. They came to the Senate together in 1926 and were serving together at the time of Senator BARKLEY's passing. I present the distinguished Senator from Arizona, Carl Hayden.

Senator HAYDEN. In my time, no one in the Congress has rendered greater service to the Nation than ALBEN BARKLEY. He has served during the administrations of seven Presidents and each one of them had high respect for his ability. I had been in the House of Representatives for a year when he came on the 4th of March 1913 as a successor to Ollie James from the Paducah district of Kentucky. Each of us came over from the House to the Senate in 1937. In the House and in the Senate ALBEN never failed to lend a helping hand when I needed his aid. By his passing I have suffered the loss of one who was always my friend.

Senator CLEMENTS. Thank you, Senator Carl Hayden.

The next voice you hear will be that of Congressman Brent Spence, from the Fifth Kentucky District.

Congressman SPENCE. The heart of the State of Kentucky is saddened today because of the death of its most distinguished citizen. Senator BARKLEY has passed away. We no longer see his genial smile or hear that musical voice which was so loved and we were pleased to listen to. He died while he was addressing a mock Democratic audience or convention in Virginia. He was a genial, clever gentleman. He was a great citizen, a great statesman, and a great patriot. He had a fine wit of love to play, not surpassed. He passed away as I know he would have liked to have gone, not from a bed of sickening and suffering but with his spirits high and with the applause and laughter of his audience ringing in his ears. He fell, as a mighty unbending oak from the forest falls before the whirlwind, and the last words were a prayer. He said, "I would rather be a servant in the house of the Lord than sit in the seats of the mighty." For over 43 years he was a faithful servant of his people, he will be a faithful servant in the house of his Lord, and the light of his Master's countenance will shine upon him I know and give him peace.

Senator CLEMENTS. Thank you, Congressman Spence.

The next voice you will hear will be that of Senator William Jenner from Indiana.

Senator JENNER. Thank you Senator Clements. As a member of the minority party in the United States Senate, I share with his Democratic colleagues a sense of grief at the passing of Senator ALBEN W. BARKLEY, of Kentucky. Senator BARKLEY, was respected by the members of the Republican Party as he was by his own party for his never failing courtesy, and good temper. He missed no opportunities to carry on political debate, but he never let party loyalty influence his respect and good will toward men with opinions different than his own. This is politics in the true American tradition. I am sure the people of Indiana sympathize with their neighbors of Kentucky at the loss of an able and devoted public servant.

Senator CLEMENTS. Thank you, Senator Jenner.

And now a voice you will hear is that of Congressman Carl Perkins from the Seventh Kentucky District.

Congressman PERKINS. Senator ALBEN BARKLEY's death is a loss to the whole world. Senator BARKLEY was a dear friend to all peace-loving nations. I, like all other Kentuckians, receive this news with the deepest of sorrow. I readily realized not only the great loss the State of Kentucky and the Nation had sustained, but the fact that we will always miss our beloved Senator. The same feeling was being expressed by every Kentuckian that I met last night in Ashland after we received the shocking news. All Kentuckians loved ALBEN BARKLEY; they loved him because he was a man of principle and an individual the ordinary laymen could look to for inspiration. It will serve no useful purpose for me to mention the outstanding and unexcelled contributions that ALBEN BARKLEY has made in the field of government except I want to say that in my judgment this country has never produced a greater public servant and statesman than Senator BARKLEY, or a man that has contributed more to the general welfare of all the people in this Nation than BARKLEY. Kentucky, as well as the Nation, has suffered this irreparable loss. Senator BARKLEY's last words, "I am willing to be a junior. I am glad to sit on the back row for I had rather be a servant in the House of the Lord than to sit in the seats of the mighty." Preceeding those words, preceding his untimely and unexpected death discloses not only his Christian qualities but that he was a man of unimpeachable integrity. I had been a close friend of ALBEN BARKLEY since 1932, just like hundreds of thousands of other Kentuckians. I recall distinctly when he first displayed his oratorical ability in my home town in Hindman in 1923 when he was a candidate for the Democratic nomination for governor. He was a companionable person which I feel is a great asset to one in public service, a public servant that you could go to for advice and always receive wise counsel. The untimely passing of Senator BARKLEY has not only aggrieved and left me with an overwhelming sense of personal loss, but has brought the same feeling to all the people of Kentucky which ALBEN BARKLEY loved with all his heart.

Senator CLEMENTS. Thank you, Congressman Perkins.

Now we will hear from a long-time friend of Senator BARKLEY's, Senator Olin Johnston, of South Carolina.

Senator JOHNSTON. Thank you, Senator Clements. ALBEN BARKLEY, the great warrior and servant of the people, has died. The void that is left in our lives in the Senate and the Democratic Party will never again be adequately filled. The great ALBEN BARKLEY will never be replaced, for when God makes men such as he, they live only once. But, we who knew ALBEN BARKLEY, and those of this generation who write history knew that ALBEN BARKLEY will never be forgotten. This imprint upon history of America will be here for as long as this Nation survives. When I was returning to Washington on the train the day he died, a hundred images of ALBEN BARKLEY passed through my mind. I saw him as a tireless warrior of the people who spent his adult lifetime fighting for the principles that serve the common everyday people of this great land. I saw him as the champion of the democratic people of this Nation. I saw ALBEN BARKLEY as a true Kentucky, southern gentleman that he was. I saw ALBEN BARKLEY, too, as he delivered his last address at the Woodrow Wilson testimonial dinner here in Washington. Perhaps I should not mention partisanship at a time like this. But ALBEN BARKLEY was a partisan man as well as a statesman. He believed in the Democratic Party. He fought for the Democratic processes and he died fighting for the same causes with unsurpassed loyalty and devotion. As we well know, with all his partisanship ALBEN BARKLEY never once faltered in determining first that whatever he decided to fight for would be in the best interests of this Nation which he loved above all else. I believe ALBEN BARKLEY was judged by a great many people as an outstanding statesman, by people everywhere long before anyone conceived of his passing away. The mightiest of the oaks of the forest has fallen. A giant among the characters of this generation has departed. Certainly nothing that any of us can say will adequately testify to what stores within us when we think of the death of ALBEN BARKLEY. As in all things we must go on. Our Nation will continue to progress. We will continue in our search for perpetual peace and freedom for this world. But none of us, no, not one, will go on in these endeavors without having first benefited because ALBEN BARKLEY lived. As we go forward together, ALBEN BARKLEY shall continue to live. Through us and those that succeeded us by the things he said, taught and did when he was among us.

Senator CLEMENTS. Thank you, Senator Johnston.

Now we will hear from a member of the Foreign Relations Committee with whom Senator BARKLEY served many years. Senator Alec Smith, of New Jersey.

Senator SMITH of New Jersey. Thank you, Senator, for your introduction. It is with great grief that I come to make this statement in behalf of my beloved friend ALBEN BARKLEY. As my friends know, I am a Republican from New Jersey. ALBEN BARKLEY was a Democrat from Kentucky, and yet from the first day I came to the Senate 12 years ago he and I have been very close. We have traveled together in foreign lands as we were both members of the Foreign Relations Committee and I have enjoyed that great friendship and that great humor and that great wit and the real kindliness of one of the great men that I have known in my life. Now, as a member of the Republican Policy Commission today at a meeting of all the Republican members of the Senate who were today in town we made a brief statement which everybody adopted by a standing vote. I offered the statement and it was adopted unanimously. The statement is as follows, which I think the public will be interested to hear:

The Republican Members of the Senate have learned with profound sorrow of the death of our beloved colleague, ALBEN BARKLEY, of Kentucky. We have admired his outstanding capacity as one of the great leaders of his party. We have respected his great talent in debate. We have enjoyed his incomparable good humor and wit, and above all, we have loved him for himself and his unfailing courtesy and thoughtful consideration of each one of us. We all extend to his wife and other members of his family our deepest sympathy and warm affection—and then the policy committee adjourned out of respect to the memory of the late Senator from Kentucky. I can only add that I feel that in the passing of Senator BARKLEY we have lost a real institution as one of our great leaders in the Senate. And even though we belonged to different parties, there's no difference between us so far as friendship, affection, and good will are concerned. ALBEN BARKLEY was a leader in developing this feeling in the Senate, this warm affection between all of us, and he has contributed enormously to the good of America, to the good of the world, and especially to the good of his friends who now mourn him so deeply.

Senator CLEMENTS. Thank you Senator Smith.

I would read now a telegram received from Congressman John C. Watts, of the Sixth Congressional District: "The death of Senator

ALBEN BARKLEY came as a profound shock to me. His living so actively amongst us for so many years gave rise to an expectancy that contemplated no end."

We will now hear from Senator Flanders of Vermont.

Senator FLANDERS. I took his words to heart, observed the senatorial processes with some care, and in time came to the conclusion that he was right. So I personally remember him for his friendliness and his personal wisdom.

Senator CLEMENTS. Thank you, Senator Flanders.

Now we will hear from Senator BARKLEY's neighbor from Indiana, Senator Homer Capehart.

Senator CAPEHART. If it were possible to gather together all the men and women who have served in the Congress of the United States since the year 1913, I am certain they would join in this unanimous statement—"We have lost a friend." That friend, of course, was certainly my good friend and yours, the distinguished and able public servant and former Vice President of the United States, Senator ALBEN W. BARKLEY. Senator BARKLEY was a man of deep conviction and sincere devotion to the political philosophy of his own party. He was at the same time a man of tremendous public stature. His long record in the Congress of the United States, extending over a period of more than 40 years, is marked with the scars of battle, for he was also an able fighter for the principles in which he believed. Thus, Senator BARKLEY frequently found himself at odds with the men privileged to serve with him in the Congress, but he was also a man who recognized the right of his most bitter opponent to his own beliefs, and the more vigor and sincerity with which they opposed him served only to increase his respect for the individual. Certainly, he was one of the most personable men ever to serve his country. His was a full life, his career a distinguished one, and his achievements for his own State and the Nation as a whole were countless. Thus, it is a sad occasion to note the passing of a good friend and a great American.

Senator CLEMENTS. Thank you, Senator Capehart.

And now I'll read a statement from Congressman Noble Gregory of the First Kentucky District:

"No one in the House or Senate had the opportunity to know Senator BARKLEY longer than I. No one had greater respect and admiration for him. His last words were dramatic, but they were typical of his life. He was a man of great strength and character. Our State, and the Nation, will miss him and his leadership."

[35]

The next voice you will hear will be that of Senator Carl Curtis, of Nebraska.

Senator CURTIS. Thank you, Senator Clements. A pillar of the Republic has fallen. ALBEN BARKLEY was the friend of all Americans. I could not add to the glory of his life or to the fine achievements that he has accomplished by enumerating them. He was a great man, a great American, a genuine friend, a devoted public servant. It was my privilege to hear him speak twice in the last week or 10 days. He was in excellent form—a fine sense of humor, a profound message and a delivery in which he put his entire personality in his speech. We have lost a great American, and while this is a time of sorrow, it is also a time when we should be grateful for the life of ALBEN W. BARKLEY.

Senator CLEMENTS. Thank you, Senator Curtis.
And now we will hear from a great friend, and one who was on the $64,000 question with Senator BARKLEY only a short time ago, Senator Carl Mundt, of South Dakota.

Senator MUNDT. Probably no man in public life more faithfully typified the position which he held than did ALBEN BARKLEY portray the living portrait of a Member of the United States Senate. If ALBEN BARKLEY had been permitted to write the drama of his own departure and to prepare his own exit lines, I am confident he would have preferred to die under circumstances precisely like those which attended his sad passing while delivering an address to a mock political convention in Virginia, yesterday. ALBEN BARKLEY was in every sense a dedicated public servant. He loved his job as he loved his country. He loved people in every walk of life, and his kindly disposition, together with his great sense of fair play, combined to make him one of the most popular figures in the current century of American public affairs. There was never anything small or petty or mean about the character of ALBEN BARKLEY. He was a big man, with a geat heart and a big concept of the public positions which he held. His passing will be mourned by Republicans and Democrats alike. America will be poorer because of his death, since his every impulse was to serve effectively the country which he loved so greatly and for which he worked so ard.

Senator CLEMENTS. Thank you, Senator Mundt.
Now we will hear from one of the younger Members of the Senate, a devoted friend of Senator BARKLEY—Senator John Kennedy, of Massachusetts.

Senator KENNEDY. I share the grief felt by the people of Kentucky at the untimely death of Senator BARKLEY. Senator BARKLEY came to Congress some years before I was born, and he was a leader and already a legendary figure when I was a schoolboy. And yet, although he held many high positions and won many great honors, majority leader, Vice President, yet at the end, when he was elected as Senator from Kentucky, he came and sat with all of us in the back row as a junior Senator, still serving the same cause he had always served in his lifetime, the State of Kentucky. Senator BARKLEY now belongs to the ages. He takes his place in the forefront of all those who have served the great State of Kentucky and the United States of America, and he will be missed by all of the people of all of the States.

Senator CLEMENTS. Thank you Senator Kennedy.

The next voice you will hear will come from the west coast, a longtime friend of our departed Kentuckian, Senator Wayne Morse, of Oregon.

Senator MORSE. One of the greatest statesmen in all America's history has fallen. ALBEN BARKLEY personified the hopes and aspirations and ideals of the Democratic Party. To millions of Americans, he not only was Mr. Democrat but he was Mr. America. ALBEN BARKLEY is irreplacable, and I think the greatest memorial we can build to him is for each one of us to try to put into practice the great spiritual leadership and ideals of this great American.

Senator CLEMENTS. Thank you, Senator Morse.

And now one whom Senator BARKLEY knew well, and where there was a very great mutual admiration, a young man in the Senate but a great friend of Senator BARKLEY's, Senator John Pastore, of Rhode Island.

Senator PASTORE. Few men in public life have ever achieved the popularity, respect, and admiration comparable to that enjoyed by Senator ALBEN W. BARKLEY. He was a vibrant, effervescent, and personable human being whom we all loved. No man had a keener understanding of our form of government, and the Nation and the free world will miss his mature judgment and experience very, very much.

Senator CLEMENTS. Thank you, Senator Pastore.

The next voice you will hear will be that of one who sat at the feet of our departed friend—Congressman William Natcher, of the Second Kentucky District.

Congressman NATCHER. Thank you, Senator Clements. At this time, I desire to pay humble tribute to the memory of my friend and fellow Kentuckian, ALBEN W. BARKLEY. His death removes from this earth one of Kentucky's greatest statesmen, and a man recognized throughout the world as a leader of men and a man of public spirit. He was a great orator and a perfect gentleman, a kind, considerate man whose exemplary life influenced his own generation and succeeding generations. Senator BARKLEY served for over 40 years in the Congress of the United States before being elected Vice President on November 2, 1948, for the term beginning January 20, 1949—a man of fine judgment, with the courage to carry out his convictions, and a true public servant. As a great Kentuckian and public servant, he again answered the call of his people after his term for Vice President expired when he was elected to the United States Senate for the term beginning January 3, 1955. Throughout his long career as a legislator, he was a friend of the farmer, the working people, small business, industry, our professions, and the veterans. In private life he gained success as a lawyer and a father. In every position he held, either private or public, he achieved distinction. His service in all of his assignments was marked by a high sense of cogency and duty. He loved people, and they in turn loved him. The qualities which endeared ALBEN W. BARKLEY to those who knew him were his devotion to his family and friends, his rugged integrity, and his unfailing sense of human and good commonsense. His contributions to better government were many and will long be remembered. The Commonwealth of Kentucky and the United States has lost a great statesman and leader. I have lost a true friend, a friend who lived his life fully and served his country well. To his wife, his children, and grandchildren, Senator ALBEN W. BARKLEY left a proud heritage. I extend to them my deepest sympathy in their bereavement.

Senator CLEMENTS. Thank you, Congressman Natcher. The next voice you will hear will be a distinguished citizen of Illinois and a long-time personal friend and great admirer of Senator BARKLEY—Senator Paul Douglas.

Senator DOUGLAS. Senator BARKLEY was probably the most beloved man in public life, and there were good reasons for this. In the first place, he was an extraordinarily witty speaker and witty in all his private and public relationships. Nearly every incident reminded him of a story, and the story was always completely fitted to the occasion. I think that Senator BARKLEY and Abraham Lincoln have probably been the two greatest storytellers in American life, and the stories which they told always illustrated principles and lighted the path to performance.

Senator BARKLEY was a kindly man. There was no malice in him, no hatred—he was a firm believer in the principles of the Democratic Party, which he know thoroughly and which he expounded on virtually every occasion which he had the chance. Well, he developed the principles of the Democratic Party and the great achievements of the Democratic Party without making personal attacks or personal reflections upon those who held opposite views or upon those in the opposite political party. He was a sturdy man, he believed firmly in the diffusion of economic and political power, he advocated those principles in legislation and on the stump. He was unfailing in their support. He knew what true democracy consisted of and he held to that. He also understood the niceties of political behavoir and of parliamentary procedure. No one was better versed than he in the way to do business and how to get legislation enacted with a minimum of friction. All in all, he was probably as fine a character as American political life has ever produced. We feel that we have suffered a great loss in his passing, but we also know that he died in about the way that he would have wanted to die, namely, with his boots on, speaking to young people about American government and about the principles of the party in which he believed. We should all be extremely grateful for his life. We have all been greatly helped by his presence, and his memory brings to us an abiding sense of the richness of American life and of the extraordinary ability of America to throw up our great leaders who espouse great principles.

Senator CLEMENTS. Thank you, Senator Douglas.

And now, from the State of New York, we will hear one who served at several levels of government and many different capacities with Senator BARKLEY—Senator Herbert Lehman, of the great Empire State.

Senator LEHMAN. The passing of ALBEN BARKLEY struck me as keen a blow as almost any I have ever experienced. His death removes from the Senate and from the national scene a towering figure whose place in history is secure beyond all the vicissitudes of time. But to us in the Senate and to me personally, this is scant consolation, for ALBEN BARKLEY was to me and to each one of us a friend, a counselor, a source of never failing wisdom, of good cheer and delight. He was a raucous strength in debate. He was a man of high principle, of undeviating loyalty to the causes in which he believed, and above all, to the welfare of his country and his people. He was bold in action, and yet moderate in his judgment. He was as courageous as a lion, yet always considerate of the views of others. He knew the meaning of compromise and concession when it was necessary to secure agreement, decision, and action. But so far as I know he never compromised on principle. Senator BARKLEY was one who, as he grew older, became even more liberal and forward-looking, thinking as much of the future as he did of the past. He had great respect for tradition, but equally great understanding of the fact that changing times required new solutions to new problems. I respected him as a statesman, but most of all I loved him as a friend. We will all miss him. There will never be another quite like him.

Senator CLEMENTS. Thank you, Senator Lehman.

The next voice you will hear will be that of the junior Senator from South Dakota, Senator Francis Case.

Senator CASE. ALBEN BARKLEY was a great American in the best traditions of greatness in America. My first contact with him was when I was a Member in the House of Representatives, and we had some legislation pending that dealt with the completion of the Mount Rushmore National Memorial out in the Black Hills of South Dakota. Mr. BARKLEY was a personal friend of Gutzon Borglum, the sculptor. He knew something of the concepts of American ideals that Borglum sought to put into the great figures he was carving out there. I had sponsored a bill in the House of Representatives, and when I came over to the Senate to get it passed there, Mr. BARKLEY was the man who helped carry it through. And then, Senator BARKLEY was a great man because he believed in preserving the integrity of the processes of democratic government. I know that as a matter of personal contact from what he has said to me personally, and only last week—the week before he passed away—the bill which he introduced was one which sought to preserve the processes of good deliberative legislation. It was a bill to provide that Members of the Senate might introduce bills only singly, not in groups, as has been a growing custom. He felt that the habit which was growing up of introducing bills with many sponsors was tending to defeat committee consideration. He made his point so clearly and effectively that when he had concluded the remarks in presenting the bill, the Senate broke out in applause. That's a rare thing in the Senate these days. It was a tribute to the greatness of Senator BARKLEY, it was a tribute to his understanding of the processes of good legislation. And so I am pleased with this opportunity to offer my few words of tribute to one of the great men of our generation and one of the great men in American history.

Senator CLEMENTS. Thank you, Senator Case.

The next voice you will hear will be that of a long-time, close personal friend from the State where our departed friend made his last statement—you will hear the voice of Senator Willis Robertson, of Virginia.

Senator ROBERTSON. In his essay on Sir Walter Scott, Thomas Carlyle, after commending the value of a healthy body, said, in effect, that the truly great man was one who possessed a healthy soul, attuned to the laws of God, as well as a healthy body, attuned to the laws of nature. During the 23 years I was privileged to know, to admire, and to learn to love ALBEN W. BARKLEY, I realized how fully he possessed those earmarks of true greatness. In all of my political career. I have never known anyone with a greater capacity for work, a greater capacity for friendship, with a greater zeal to promote the cause of good government. To those of us who intimately knew him, who worked with him, who loved him, his sudden passing is a great blow. But what could be more typical of a healthy soul, attuned to the laws of God, than his words "I would rather be a servant in the House of the Lord than to sit in the seats of the mighty." Senator BARKLEY believed that life goes down with better grace, foaming in full body over a precipice, than miserably straggling to an end in sandy deltas. Therefore, in ending his distinguished career in the type of work which he loved best, death was robbed of its sting and the grave of its victory.

Senator CLEMENTS. Thank you, Senator Willis Robertson.

The next voice will be that of one who served intimately with Senator BARKLEY for many years in the Senate. They were on committees together, and they functioned together in the interest of the American people for many years—Senator Joe O'Mahoney, of Wyoming.

Senator O'MAHONEY. For more than 20 years, I was associated with Senator ALBEN W. BARKLEY in the United States Senate. I speak of him as a friend and as a man. When I think of him, and it shall be often—indeed, until, I, too, pass from the scene—I shall think of a man of character, a man of ability, a man of great personal strength, a man of wisdom and of rare good humor. He had the common touch, he knew that this was a people's government. I often heard him speak of the fact that Abraham Lincoln was among his heroes. He had the same characteristics that Lincoln had of being able to illustrate an argument with a humorous story. And the stories he told were stories that all could hear. I'm sorry, indeed, that it becomes my sad duty to participate in this memorial. The people of Kentucky have lost a great friend and a great statesman. The people of the United States have lost one of the greatest champions of public liberty and of the welfare of the masses of the people. ALBEN BARKLEY was among the great figures in our congressional government.

Senator CLEMENTS. Thank you, Senator O'Mahoney.

Now the next voice you will hear will be that of the junior Senator from Iowa—Senator Thomas Martin.

Senator MARTIN. Thank you, Senator Clements. Senator ALBEN WILLIAM BARKLEY established an amazing record of service to his State of Kentucky and to our Nation throughout his entire lifetime. His record of service in the House of Representatives, in the Senate, and as Vice President, was an inspiration to all of us in Congress. He was in a position of great leadership when I first came to Congress in January 1939, and he continued his leadership to the last moment of his life. His good influence went far beyond partisan lines always. During my brief service in the United States Senate since January 1955, I have appreciated the opportunity to work closer with him. I have been better able to observe his leadership in Senate proceedings, and I have come to know him and understand his great qualities of character and devotion to the cause of good government. His good qualities will live on in all of us who were privileged to know him and work with him. I join with my colleagues in extending to his family my deepest sympathy in their bereavement.

Senator CLEMENTS. Thank you, Senator Martin.

And now to bring this program to a close I want to present a young man from the Fourth Congressional District in Kentucky, one who knew and loved our distinguished friend who has passed on, one who had an intimate relationship with him throughout the Congressman's experience both at the county level and at the national level of Government. I know the affection that existed between the two. I present to you to conclude this program— Congressman from the Fourth Congressional District in Kentucky— Frank Chelf.

Congressman CHELF. Senator Clements, this is a sad day for Paducah. A sorrowful day for McCracken County, an unhappy day for all of Kentucky, and a horrible blow for the Nation and the

[42]

world. We, as you know down in Kentucky have lost not only a great man, an outstanding citizen, a foremost American, an extraordinary legislator but one of the finest, one of the sweetest, one of the most lovable persons who ever walked under the broad, blue canopy of God's own heaven. Earle, I could go on and on and on and say what's on my mind and down deep in my heart but suffice it to say that we have lost a great American. I would like to say to you that when he came down to campaign in my great Fourth Congressional District back in 1954, that I went with him on every stump-speaking tour. Yes, as you know, Earle, we campaigned together. And you campaigned with him, too, and hard, and you were most effective, my dear friend. Yes, we had fun—to be with him was to have fun. He was a wonderful companion of yours and of mine and you and I liked to call him our dear friend and our buddy. To show you, Earle, how considerate he was of others—I don't have to tell you, my friend, but you know, but for those who don't really know—I suspect they do, but in case they don't, when I was campaigning with him, he often told me, Earle, that I shouldn't work so hard, making so many speeches for him. He'd say to me, Frank, you have no opposition at all either in your primary or in your general election. You are just out of the hospital and major surgery. Take it easy, my boy. It was an inspiration just to be with him, Earle, as you know. And when he wasn't looking, bless his heart, I'd hold my side and my scars and proceed to pour it on as best I could for him. Thank heaven, he carried my great district over 10,000 votes. And, Earle, he carried your great, old Second Congressional District by the proverbial gillion or better. He has so conducted himself amongst his fellow men, he has let his light so shine that his fellow men might see his good works and glorify our Father who is in heaven. He has created with his own hands, Earle, his high station in life. He has built a monument higher, brighter, whiter, and more beautiful, if you please, than the Washington Monument itself. I rather suspect that the Master will say, "Well done, thou good and faithful servant. Enter into the kingdom above." And Earle, I know you loved him, I know all Kentuckians loved him. And God rest his soul in peace, and I know this, that somewhere, somehow way out there beyond the blue the old massa will have a special place in that great mansion of rest.

Mr. KNOWLAND. Mr. President, it was with profound sorrow that the Senate learned of the passing of ALBEN BARKLEY. He had served his State and his Nation well. He was a vigorous partisan, but not a bitter one.

Those of us who have had the privilege—and it was a high privilege—to have served in the Senate with ALBEN BARKLEY have happy memories which can never be taken from us.

I remember when I first came to the Senate, 11 years ago, I had an association with ALBEN BARKLEY because he had served in the House of Representatives with my father some 40 years before.

Senator BARKLEY was always kindly. I marveled at the work he did as majority leader of the Senate. I have never known an occupant of that office who worked harder in the interests of his country and his party than ALBEN BARKLEY.

Some of us knew of the heavy family burden he was carrying because of the illness of his wife, who subsequently died. Yet ALBEN BARKLEY was at his post of duty in the Senate and always faithfully performed the onerous duties of the majority leadership.

He had a distinguished record as a Member of the House of Representatives, and a distinguished and long record in the Senate. He was elevated to the high office of Vice President of the United States, and, as such, he served as Presiding Officer of the Senate for more than 4 years. He temporarily retired into private life, but within 2 years the people of Kentucky had called their son back once again to represent them in the Senate.

I am sure all remaining Members of the Senate share a feeling of great personal loss because of the death of Senator BARKLEY, and all of us know that no man on either side of the aisle commanded greater respect among his colleagues than did our late, beloved colleague, ALBEN BARKLEY.

Mr. President, I speak for the members of the minority, and we extend to his family, to his friends, and to the State of Kentucky our deepest sympathy in the loss of a great man. The Nation and the Senate can ill afford such a loss.

Mr. PAYNE. Mr. President, the entire Nation has joined in mourning the death of ALBEN W. BARKLEY. His passing leaves a void in the Senate and on the national scene which will not be easily filled. It has been a high personal privilege and honor for me to serve in this body beside the Vice President who administered my senatorial oath of office in January 1953. As evidence of the high esteem in which the State of Maine held Senator BARKLEY, I ask unanimous consent that five representative editorials from Maine newspapers may be printed at this point in the body of the Record.

There being no objection, the editorials were ordered to be printed in the Record, as follows:

[From the Portland (Maine) Press Herald of May 2, 1956]

A GREAT OLD SOLDIER REFUSED TO FADE AWAY

Basically, it was Senator BARKLEY's durability that brought a long parade of nonpartisan mourners to his bier.

His humor was durable. Neither classic nor subtle, it was devoid of all the sham and posturing of the comedian. His sense of fair play was durable, at times spectacularly so, as was the case when he angrily resigned his majority leadership in protest against another fairly regular Democrat, President Franklin D. Roosevelt, after the latter vetoed a tax bill BARKLEY had worked hard to get enacted.

His contagious faith in his party's fortunes found him in 1948, through the sheer power of his rich convention oratory, lifting fading Democratic hopes to new heights. Nor was a genuine faith in his own destiny any less. Others laughed when BARKLEY wanted to be President in 1952, but the Senator was dead serious. The laughers were quieted by the sight of BARKLEY's obvious grief on being informed he was too old, returning to their corners in mute respect 2 years later as the smiling warrior campaigned successfully for his old seat in the United States Senate.

The loyal Barkleys are the fiber of which sound two-party government is made. Neither statesman nor scholar, he possessed a quality—durability of purpose and principle—essential to statesmanship and without which no scholar can win more than momentary acclaim.

[From the Bangor (Maine) Daily News of May 2, 1956]

AN ABLE AND BELOVED MAN DIES

A colorful, hard-working figure has been removed from the American political stage by the death of Senator ALBEN W. BARKLEY.

[45]

The popular Kentucky Democrat held varied and prominent roles during his 43-year career in Washington. He started out as a Congressman in 1913, later became a Senator and majority leader, served under Truman as Vice President, and then in 1954 went back to the Senate as the junior Member from Kentucky.

The Kentuckian, who started life as a farm boy, developed into a spellbinding orator. He could convulse banquet audiences with humorous yarns or hush the Senate Chamber with solemn, emotion-packed speeches. He was one of his party's best campaigners.

Senator BARKLEY served the late President Roosevelt loyally throughout the New Deal era. They had one public dispute. This occurred when BARKLEY felt that Roosevelt had criticized the integrity of Congress in a tax-veto message. Here BARKLEY was caught between two loyalties—to his President and to his Senate colleagues. Roosevelt's famed "Dear Alben" letter smoothed out the row, and at the Democratic convention soon afterward BARKLEY nominated Roosevelt for his fourth term.

BARKLEY's influence continued under Truman. As Vice President he was too colorful and valuable to remain in the background. He became known as the Veep and toiled hard as Truman's right-hand man.

He was affectionately termed from time to time the party's "wheelhorse" and "warhorse." These he was—a loyal, industrious, and popular politician. The Democrats were counting heavily on him as an adviser and as a campaigner in the current presidential campaign.

His political wisdom and vigor will be sorely missed by his party. The man himself will be missed by the Nation.

[From the Lewiston (Maine) Sun of May 2, 1956]

SENATOR ALBEN BARKLEY

When Senator ALBEN BARKLEY told a student audience, just before he was struck down on Monday by a fatal heart attack, that he had rather "be a servant in the house of the Lord than sit in the seat of the mighty," he may have been paraphrasing a briefer and better well-known political quotation.

He may have been thinking, with reference to his long and honorable career, that he had "rather be right than President." For Senator BARKLEY might have been President had he not tried so hard to be right. In 1944 he fought unsuccessfully, as Senate majority leader to salvage the late President Roosevelt's tax program. But the Chief Executive stingingly vetoed the bill Congress finally approved, and inferentially rebuked BARKLEY as well. Observers at Washington believe this break in their long friendship led Roosevelt to choose Truman as his Vice Presidential running mate in the fourth term campaign of that year.

Senator BARKLEY was a man of great wit and charm, assets that served him well during 7 terms in the House of Representatives, beginning in 1913, and nearly 4 terms in the Senate, from which he resigned to run successfully with Harry Truman in 1948. After a half-hearted effort to win the presidential nomination in 1952— the powerful labor unions turned thumbs down, he was returned to the Senate. More than a politician, Senator ALBEN BARKLEY was almost an American institution, and though his great days were behind him, he will be missed.

[From the Rockland (Maine) Courier-Gazette of May 3, 1956]

VALE, VEEP

Today we join the Nation in expressing our sorrow at the passing of one of America's most beloved personalities, ALBEN W. BARKLEY, the gentleman from Kentucky.

From the humble background of a farm in his native State he advanced, step by step, to a prominent place in the National Government, the No. 2 spot, Vice President, in the latest Democratic administration. Beginning his political carreer in 1905 as county attorney, he worked his way through the State legislature, the United States House of Representatives, the United States Senate, finally became Veep, an alphabetical contraction of Vice President, which he coined himself and which his successor in the distinguished office was courteous enough to decline to accept, feeling that it was distinctly Mr. BARKLEY's own title.

First of all a loyal American, BARKLEY was next a Democrat, with a capital D. Party loyalty was the only way of political life he understood but never did he permit his party affiliation to surpass his firm belief in the Constitution of the United States and in the rights we were granted as citizens of this Nation. When in 1944 his great and good friend, President Franklin D. Roosevelt, attempted to exceed his Presidential powers by directing congressional action on tax legislation BARKLEY had the courage to oppose him. Rather than to support the administration's aim he resigned as majority leader of the Senate, an action that required much courage. Be it ever to the credit of our country that this forceful manner of calling attention to things that should not be resulted in a change of attitude by the President and in the unanimous reelection of Mr. BARKLEY to the office from which he had resigned in protest.

He died as he would want to if he could have been given a choice, addressing a group of college students assembled in mock Democratic convention, to learn all they could of the intricacies of our National Government.

Through the miracle of television the Nation was permitted to see his last appearance on the platform and hear his last sentence, one which may well be his epitaph. It describes most truthfully the entire life of this great man:

"I had rather be a servant in the house of the Lord than to sit in the seats of the mighty."

Vale, Veep!

[From the Bangor (Maine) Patriot of May 2, 1956]

THE BELOVED VEEP

It is not an exaggeration to say that hardly a home in these United States but felt the loss of a member when ALBEN W. BARKLEY dropped dead on the political platform at Washington and Lee University in Lexington, Va., Monday evening.

BARKLEY had become endeared to Americans as the beloved Veep. So much so, that Richard M. Nixon, a man nearly half his age upon succeeding him as Vice President of the United States, made as his first request that no one call him the Veep. That title, Nixon rightly said, had become hallowed by BARKLEY.

The qualities that made BARKLEY so widely beloved were bred on a Kentucky farm, from which he sprang; his humanity and humor, his humility and perseverance, and his sense of identity with the comman man, which was never lost though he sat in national councils. He was leader of the Senate majority for more years than any other man, Vice President of the United States and a potential candidate for his party's nomination for President.

There was another man, also born in Paducah, Ky., who became beloved of his fellow Americans. He was the humorist, Irvin S. Cobb. Sixteen months BARKLEY's senior, Cobb in his writing and BARKLEY in his speaking, made Paducah known as the font of good, clean American humor. Their like are hard to come by any more. They were part of the postfrontier America.

BARKLEY's last words were an eloquent testimony of his virtues. He could not have shaped a better introduction had he known they would be the words heard by Saint Peter as he knocked for admittance at the pearly gate. He had just reviewed in brief his political career—Congressman, junior Senator, senior Senator, majority leader, Vice President, and again junior Senator. Then he added:

"I am willing to be a junior. I am glad to sit on the back row, for I had rather be a servant in the House of the Lord than to sit in the seats of the mighty."

Mr. ELLENDER. Mr. President, many of our great Americans were born of poor and humble parents. Most of those who climbed highest on the shining ladder of fame commenced at the lowest round. Some of them were self-made; they took advantage of every opportunity to obtain an education even by doing chores while attending school. ALBEN BARKLEY was one of these. He was one of those great Americans, in some respects like our own Jefferson, Jackson, and Lincoln, to name but a few, whose names have all the luster of a star. Because of the death of ALBEN BARKLEY, I know that in every household across this land there is sorrow and a feeling of great personal loss.

I doubt that there ever has been a man who captured the hearts of Americans the way ALBEN BARKLEY did during his long and valuable tenure in public life. He was best known as the "Veep," a name given him by his grandchildren, but which was soon universally adopted. This endearing title was typical of the feeling held for ALBEN BARKLEY by all Americans—it denoted respect, regard, and a great affection.

ALBEN BARKLEY was an "old hand" when I came to the Senate in 1937. His service in this body began in 1927. Before being elected to the Senate, he served as a prosecuting attorney, a county judge, and later a Member of the House of Representatives. After 1948 he served as Vice President of the United States and President of the Senate with great distinction.

ALBEN BARKLEY left us in 1952; there were people who said he had retired from public life. The "Veep" could never retire, not so long as his great heart pumped life through his courageous body. He returned to the Senate only last year.

He took a seat on the rear row, as must all Senators who are junior in term of continuous service. The Congressional Directory for this year lists ALBEN BARKLEY as No. 44 in term of service. That may be statistically correct, but I am sure that to us, his colleagues, he was always No. 1.

He had a front seat in the hearts of those of us who had known him, worked with him, toiled long hours with him over legislation in which we had mutual interests. It is an understatement to say that we will miss ALBEN BARKLEY. We will do more than that, for the "Veep" was not only a colleague and a Senator, he was a friend and an adviser, ready and able to advise all who desired counsel; he was always unselfish in sharing the knowledge that experience had brought. He was a philosopher, a man dedicated to the proposition that a government must not direct, but serve the people. He was a great Democrat, a great American, a great statesman. He was the last of that vanishing breed of statesman who brought the Senate of the United States to its present eminence, and who helped vest it with the title of the world's greatest deliberative body.

Death must come to all of us, at some time. It is inevitable, something we cannot avoid and something about which we frequently do not give much thought. I wonder, though, if many or any of us will have the privilege of meeting death as we would most like. I cannot believe that ALBEN BARKLEY could have chosen a better opportunity to depart this life than that which fate directed for him. He was doing that which he best liked to do—instructing young Ameicans in the fundamentals of our national existence. He was speaking from a platform, imparting to those gathered to hear his words some of the wisdom with which long years of experience had enriched him.

ALBEN BARKLEY, and those other great Senators who have gone before, have left us a precious political heritage; the Veep has presented this Chamber and the Nation with a great legacy in his fundamental political philosophy; Senator

BARKLEY, the man, has moulded and left for generations yet unborn a long and glowing record of service, patriotism, and devotion to the cause of the public good.

Even today, as we mourn his loss, I hope that all of us will remember that there is a greater wreath which we may yet lay upon ALBEN BARKLEY's memory—and that is the promise that in the months and years ahead, we will strive to live up to the ideals and standards he left behind.

Mr. FREAR. Mr. President, there are many Members of this great body and of the House of Representatives whose friendship and association with the late Senator BARKLEY, from Kentucky, goes back for many, many years.

Thus, they can and will recall in their remarks some of the great legislative acts of earlier days in which he played so distinguished and prominent a part.

I can refer only to the more recent period, from 1949 until the present, but in that brief span of time, I have never enjoyed a more real and lasting friendship than that which I was privileged to share with Senator Barkley.

In 1949 at my request he came to Delaware to address one of the most successful Jefferson-Jackson Day dinners ever conducted in my State. His message, filled with the characteristic BARKLEY spirit and colorful phasing, won him an immediate host of new friends from the First State.

Subsequently, he returned for another dinner in 1953 and campaigned in the State both for my election and for that of some of my colleagues.

With him on later occasions, he brought his charming and lovely wife.

Here at the Senate both during his tenure as Vice President and later when he returned to the Senate itself, I have enjoyed many unforgettable moments listening to his almost endless and delightful wealth of anecdotes for which he was so justly famous.

On more serious occasions I have counseled with him frequently on legislative matters of the greatest importance.

His knowledge and understanding of the process of legislation were virtually unbounded.

Mr. President, on the day before his death, it was the pleasure of Mrs. Frear and me to be with the BARKLEYS at dinner at the home of Senator and Mrs. Byrd, and as usual he was concerned with legislative matters pending before the Finance Committee and was looking forward to a resumption of committee activities later in the week.

I could not help thinking, Mr. President, as we traveled from Washington to Paducah last Wednesday that although this Nation has produced many great men during its short span of history, few have equaled the overall stature of Senator BARKLEY.

For he was an individual who could as easily walk with the humble as with the mighty.

His neighbors of many years who lined the streets of his hometown en route to his final resting place gave evidence of their warm and respected feeling for their departed friend.

Mr. President, this Chamber has lost one of the most able and gracious personalities that has ever sat in the Senate of the United States.

I shall miss him most deeply both as a friend and as a colleague but his family, his State, and the Nation can take assurance from the fact that he has indelibly carved for himself a place in our Nation's history that will ever remain as one of lasting honor.

Mr. BRIDGES. Mr. President, in the death of our distinguished colleague, ALBEN BARKLEY, the American people have lost a devoted servant. His sudden and tragic passing has silenced a courageous voice and stilled a fighting heart.

I feel a deep and very personal sorrow in Senator BARKLEY's departure from our midst. Since I came to the Senate in 1937, I held a deep respect for him and considered him a true, personal friend. We differed many times on political and legislative issues, but in my experience here in Washington he has been fair on his approach to those differences. His vast experience in public life kept him close to the minor as well as the major problems facing the American people for close to a half century.

The life of ALBEN BARKLEY should serve as a model for America's boyhood. He was born of poor parents in a small log cabin, and he worked the soil to help his struggling family. He worked as a janitor to earn his way through college, and became a lawyer.

Since 1905, when he was elected a county prosecutor, he fought tirelessly for what he considered to be the welfare of the American people. He came to Congress in 1913, and during the intervening 43 years devoted his mind and his heart and his body to the Nation. The Nation rewarded him in 1948 by electing him to the second highest office in the land—the Vice Presidency. Back in 1937 he was elected majority leader of the Senate, and for 11 years carried this tremendous burden on his shoulders.

The people of Kentucky gave to the American people a man of whom they could justly be proud. His actions, his words of wisdom, and his great sense of humor will long be remembered. I have a sincere sympathy for Mrs. Barkley in these sorrowful days, but she must be strengthened in her unfortunate loss by the fact that during his lifetime ALBEN BARKLEY made a tremendous contribution to the welfare of the Nation he loved so deeply.

Mr. President, at a regular meeting of the Republican policy committee of the Senate, on Tuesday, May 1, 1956, which was attended by a large number of other Republican Senators, the following resolution of sorrow was adopted unanimously, following which the policy committee adjourned out of respect to the memory of the late Senator from Kentucky:

The Republican Members of the Senate have learned with profound sorrow of the death of our beloved colleague, ALBEN BARKLEY, of Kentucky.

We have admired his outstanding capacity as one of the great leaders of his party; we have respected his great talent in debate; we have enjoyed his incomparable good humor and wit; but, above all, we have loved him for himself and for his unfailing courtesy and thoughtful consideration of each one of us.

We all extend to his wife and other members of his family our deepest sympathies and warm affection.

Mr. STENNIS. Mr. President, certainly on an occasion when tributes are offered to the memory of the late ALBEN BARKLEY every Senator would want to express his very strong, deep, and abiding sentiments. However, I find myself today among those who are not prepared to express my sentiments on short notice.

Mr. CLEMENTS. Mr. President, will the Senator yield?

Mr. STENNIS. I yield.

Mr. CLEMENTS. I can assure my friend from Mississippi— at least, I can, and a little earlier today, I did express my personal view—that a day will be set aside in the near future, after proper notice has been given, when Senators may offer their expressions of sympathy and tribute with respect not only to the distinguished former Vice President and distinguished former Member of the Senate who has passed on, but also at the same time may offer their expressions with reference to the distinguished former senior Senator from West Virginia, Mr. KILGORE.

I should think that some details with reference to the selection of a time which would be suitable to the members of the families of the deceased Senators would have to be arranged; but I may say to my friend from Mississippi that there are those of us who had such sentiments in our hearts and felt compelled to express them today.

Mr. STENNIS. I appreciate the assurance given by the distinguished Senator from Kentucky that a day for the offering of tributes to the memories of the deceased Senators will be set aside. I also fully appreciate the fact that today was an appropriate day for any Senator who felt prepared to do so to express his sentiments.

I am very glad to know, Mr. President, that an occasion will be afforded all Senators to pay tribute to the late, departed ALBEN BARKLEY, and also to our colleague, the Senator from West Virginia, Mr. KILGORE. I had thoughts of Senator KILGORE also on my mind and had intended to mention them. However, I am glad to learn that a day in memoriam will be set aside, after, as the acting majority leader has suggested, having consulted with the families of the deceased Senators.

Mr. MANSFIELD. Mr. President, I join with my colleagues in the Senate in expressing deep regret upon the passing of our late friend, the Senator from Kentucky, Mr. BARKLEY.

It has been a privilege for me to sit at Senator BARKLEY's right hand in the back row, because he has been very free with his advice; and to a younger Member of the Senate he, of course, has been an inspiration.

As a Member of the House and Senate, I have known ALBEN BARKLEY for 14 years. I think of him as a man of sterling integrity, wise counsel, and great ability. I know we shall miss him, and miss him deeply, because in addition to being a statesman, he was also a man of humor and profound understanding.

I feel quite certain that our late colleague is now serving in the ranks of those with whom he was associated. I am certain he is enjoying his true reward. No matter where ALBEN BARKLEY is, I am certain he will keep his eye on this Chamber and make sure, so far as he can, that we do a good job for the country and the free world.

Mr. HUMPHREY. Mr. President, like the Senator from Mississippi [Mr. Stennis], at a later day, when the time has been set aside for the presentation of memorials to the late Senator from Kentucky, Mr. BARKLEY, and the late Senator from West Virginia, Mr. KILGORE, I shall, of course, want to participate.

But today we have been afforded an opportunity to say a few words about our beloved friend and colleague, that great American, the late Senator from Kentucky, Mr. BARKLEY, and I want to share in that opportunity.

It was my privilege to go to Paducah, Ky., and to attend the funeral service and last rites for Senator BARKLEY. Anyone who made that trip and witnessed the hundreds, yes thousands, of persons along the streets of the communities through which our train passed, would have recognized, again and again, the great love, affection, and admiration felt by the people of Kentucky for Senator BARKLEY. I was deeply moved by their demonstration of sorrow. I was particularly impressed when I saw the large numbers of young persons, including schoolchildren, in community after community, who watched reverently as our train moved along. Those young persons stood in respectful silence, paying mute tribute to the great leader and honored statesman from Kentucky.

The people of Paducah demonstrated their heartfelt affection for ALBEN BARKLEY. It was a touching and moving experience for those of us who were there to extend our sympathy to his family and friends.

Mr. President, ALBEN BARKLEY was a good friend of Minnesota, and the people of Minnesota loved him. He had been in our State many times, both on political business and on missions of civic participation. I recall his coming to Minnesota in 1948. I recall his visit to the Minneapolis Aquatenial celebration in 1949. I recall his visit to Duluth, Minn., in 1951. On other times, as Senator and as Vice President, he shared with us his profound knowledge of politics, and, above all, his qualities of kindness, understanding, and friendliness.

ALBEN BARKLEY lived life to the fullest extent. He had the privilege of knowing President Wilson as a friend and as an associate in government. He served during the most critical years of his country's history. That period included World War I and the postwar period of the 1920's. He was a stalwart figure in the Senate in the 1930's, the leader of many of the programs known as the New Deal, the right arm of Franklin Delano Roosevelt. In the Second World War years his responsibility as majority leader was again a testimonial to his qualities of statesmanship and patriotism.

In the postwar years after World War II, Senator BARKLEY had as much to do with formulating congressional policies relating to our foreign relations and foreign policy as had any other Member of Congress, and probably more than most.

His services as Vice President endeared him to everyone. I think it was a fine demonstration of respect for ALBEN BARKLEY when our present Vice President made it quite clear that the unique title of "Veep" was to be reserved only for ALBEN BARKLEY.

The Korean war period was a difficult one for all of us. Senator BARKLEY, then Vice President, rendered great service, by going to Korea and to Western Europe, strengthening our alliances, and promoting understanding everywhere he went.

Mr. President, this is but a thumbnail sketch of what many of us think and recall.

Senator BARKLEY's return to the Senate in 1955 could, I think, be described as the highlight of his career. Here was a man who had participated in all levels of government, legislative and executive, a man from the soil, a man from humble parentage. He could have rested on his laurels, but he wanted to come back to the Chamber that meant so much to him, and he came back in full health and spirit, wise, prudent, generous, and kindly.

The Senate is a better Senate because ALBEN BARKLEY was here. He will always be here.

I conclude, Mr. President, by saying one of the great privileges of public service is the opportunity to know men like ALBEN BARKLEY. One of the finest honors which can come to anyone is to have one of the stature and character of ALBEN BARKLEY call him friend. I shall ever be grateful that it was my privilege to share in his friendship. America can be ever grateful that a man by the name of ALBEN BARKLEY lived and worked and died for his country.

Mr. President, I ask unanimous consent to have printed in the Record at this point two editorials, one of which appeared in the Minneapolis Star and Tribune, and the other of which appeared in the St. Paul Pioneer Press and Dispatch, pertaining to the loss and the death of our beloved friend, the late Senator BARKLEY.

There being no objection, the editorials were ordered to be printed in the Record, as follows:

[From the Minneapolis Star and Tribune]

THE VEEP IS GONE

Few persons in public life have been as widely loved as ALBEN BARKLEY. The reason is plain—few possessed the talent he had for tolerance, friendliness, courtesy, and good humor.

He was Vice President in a tense period, yet none of the often sharp charges and countercharges of those years originated with him or were directed at him. He was a stalwart party man, yet his personal charm and urbane oratory reached easily across party lines.

Politics treated him well and he treated politics well. He said he wanted to stay in the game the rest of his life—and so he did. Death no doubt came to him as he would have wished.

There is not with his passing the sense of loss of an irreplaceable figure in some great public issue. But Senator BARKLEY had even rarer qualities and the entire Nation grieves at the departure of a fine Kentucky gentleman.

———

[From the St. Paul Pioneer Press and Dispatch]

SENATOR BARKLEY

Only the American South can bring out a political career like that of Senator BARKLEY, and perhaps even there it will not be possible much longer. But only a personality with his combination of wisdom, humor, and strength could have made the particular kind of career in public life he did. He has died at 78 literally with his political boots on, and this is not much of a coincidence since he had them on most of the time.

His public life was for all practical purposes solely in Congress, since even when he was Vice President his real role was in the

Senate over which he presided. His contributions were not those of great imagination in legislation, for no outstanding creations of statesmanship stand in his name. Neither was he any flaming crusader for causes. But he was a wise, warm, and witty gentleman whose fund of experience in the ways of Congress and Washington was not exceeded by that of any man of his time.

Even in other English-speaking countries, where the ins and outs of a two-party system are familiar, the Barkleys of American politics are somewhat of a marvel and enigma. History accounts for but fails logically to explain the paradox of the combination in a single party of northern liberals with southern conservatives— a combination which has had its troubles and is having them now but which nevertheless has persisted with astonishing smoothness for a long time.

The key to the riddle is personal, and BARKLEY and his politics are the best example. He was majority leader of the Senate during a time when his southern colleagues and the second administration of Roosevelt's New Deal were mostly at odds. No one would have predicted it would work out but by and large it did. Anywhere else that would have been politically the end of BARKLEY but in a sense it was just another beginning for him.

Senator BARKLEY is perhaps typical of American ability to make diversity on the grand scale come together in an acceptable national unity.

Mr. HUMPHREY. Mr. President, I am sure these editorials represent the affection and sympathy which the people of Minnesota had for Senator BARKLEY and for his family.

Mr. MORSE. Mr. President, one of the great statesmen in America's entire history fell when ALBEN BARKLEY died. In the hearts and in the affections of millions of his countrymen, ALBEN BARKLEY not only was Mr. Democrat, but he was Mr. America. And I would say that the greatest monument we can build to his memory is for each one of us to try to put into our living the ideals and the aspirations and the spiritual values that dominated his life.

The Senator from Minnesota [Mr. Humphrey] has referred to the great tribute which was paid to Senator BARKLEY at his funeral in Paducah, Ky., when, as we drove the miles from the church to the cemetery, the roadway for the entire distance was lined with thousands of Americans who loved him. I was told children came great distances to stand in reverent respect to the memory of this great American. Many white and colored citizens of the great State of Kentucky were as one with bowed heads, as they paid their last respects to this fallen statesman.

Mr. President, I think one of the most beautiful eulogies I have ever had the privilege of hearing—and it is just as beautiful in reading—is the one the Chaplain of the Senate paid Senator BARKLEY in the literary form of a magnificent prayer at the funeral service held at Foundry Methodist Church in Washington, D. C. It is such a fitting tribute and eulogy to this great statesman that, by association, I would make it mine, as my verbal tribute to ALBEN BARKLEY. It is a prayer, the reading of which, in my judgment, will make us better men and women.

So, Mr. President, in all humility, I read the Chaplain's great prayer:

O Thou Master of all good workmen: We come to Thy sanctuary this hour with a sense of poignant loss, vividly conscious of an empty place against the sky, at which our surprised eyes are staring, stunned, bewildered, and strangely moved. We sit together in the sadness of farewell as we mourn the sudden passing from our sight and side of one of the greatest of our national leaders—for there is a prince and a great man fallen. One of the Republic's best-loved sons—Thy servant across toiling years in all great and good causes— ALBEN W. BARKLEY.

From our partial, finite point of view, his State and the Nation, which he served with such unstinted devotion, are vastly poorer because his eloquent, passionate voice will be heard no more in its councils, on its platforms, and in its national forums. For us, there is an altered world since but a few hours ago he "went down in full armor," with unabated powers, having lived his strenuous years up to the hilt. He so numbered his days, applying his heart unto wisdom, because to him the whole earth was the house of the Lord, as echoed by the last phrase which fell from his lips.

And now we come in gratitude to think tenderly of one who occupied high office, and yet never stooped to low designs; who was greatly honored by his countrymen, but who ever put principle above pedestal; who was a partisan, with deep convictions, yet without a blind spot that cannot see the integrity of an opponent's position.

We exalt the memory this hour of one who walked with kings nor lost the common touch, who could remain silent under unjust attack—as he often did—exemplifying that "he who keepeth his own spirit is greater than he who taketh a city."

We think of one who with unbowed head and unembittered heart met life's losses, and who found constant fun in living, and who reveled in laughter; who loved folks more than fortune, and who was valiant as a knight of old, in righting wrongs and enthroning justice; and who counted it as a part of his religion to help see that his country was well governed.

While we mourn that we shall see his face no more, solemnize us by the uncertainty of our own working day. May we lengthen our brief span by intensity of living, filling swift hours with mighty deeds. If there is any kindness we can show, may we not neglect nor defer it—seeing that we pass this way but once.

And thus, at last, O Lord of the living and of the living dead, bring us all to the Homeland or Thine eternal love. We ask it through riches of grace in Christ Jesus our Lord. Amen.

Mr. McNAMARA. Mr. President, as one whose life has been greatly enriched by Senator BARKLEY, I should like to be associated with the remarks of the Senator from Kentucky [Mr. Clements] and the other Members of the Senate who have spoken here today in memory of Senator BARKLEY.

I know that Senator BARKLEY had great admiration and personal respect for many of his colleagues in this body. He constantly referred to them as great Americans. I am sure that on Thursday May 3, we laid to rest in his beloved State of Kentucky the greatest of these great Americans.

Mr. President, while I have the floor, on behalf of the junior Senator from Rhode Island [Mr. Pastore], I ask unanimous consent that a statement prepared by him expressing his sentiments about the passing of the late Senator BARKLEY be printed in the Record.

There being no objection, the statement was ordered to be printed in the Record, as follows:

STATEMENT BY SENATOR PASTORE

A seat of the mighty is truly vacant with the passing of a servant in the House of the Lord.

ALBEN BARKLEY was a servant, too, in the homes of his people. And his people were not limited to the loyal confines of the Kentucky to which he was devoted—nor to the limits of these United States to which he was dedicated. For his love and labor for neighbor touched the humble and the hopeless of the whole world, as his patriotic leadership accepted our responsibilities toward a world that would be free.

ALBEN BARKLEY was a servant, too, in the hearts of his colleagues. Each of us has his own debt of gratitude to the genial, generous statesman who will be at our call and counsel no more. We would strive to express our sentiments in phrases simple enough to match the humility of our gracious companion in these halls—though our emotions seek to find the golden eloquence of words to measure the achievements of this worker and warrior for peace on earth and good will among men.

My personal indebtedness to ALBEN BARKLEY is partly in the written records of this body—his appointments to place and position—as he started a fledgling Senator toward increasing duties and distinctions.

But the true values of his inspiration are written where no other man can read—and where I could not and would not erase them—from the tablets of my heart.

To me the prize was not so much the position itself, but the evidence of the confidence of this great man in the possibilities of this new-come Senator—new come from beginnings as lowly as his own, but enflamed by the enthusiasms, the inspiration, the encouragement of this magnificent mind that could find time for this humble Pastore, anxious to be a credit to his people and to the traditions of this position for which they had chosen him.

I dare to speak thus intimately here, because I know that in the experience of many of you are these same unforgettable memories of a good man and a great friend.

Indeed, his friendship semed to be so personal a possession to us that we had forgotten—almost—that we shared it with countless thousands—yes, millions—who looked upon ALBEN BARKLEY as their friend.

It is one of the revelations of these days of sorrowful headlines that every sector of our country is eager to recall some local and intimate incident—some speech or visit—that so ties ALBEN BARKLEY to their relationship—that he is the common possession of our great land.

Kentucky claims him. Washington proclaims him. But every vale and hamlet from shore to shore possesses him. And well they might. For the record of his deeds is the creed of our country in the most critical era of its existence. Part of his will and testament to the American people is the tremendous social legislation of the thirties—sponsored and spearheaded in large measure by him—from ideals to actualities.

To the world at large his leadership of lend-lease and his work for the ratification of the United Nations Charter can never be omitted from any history which shall record the hopes of mankind.

All history will be the richer for the virtues, the voice, and the vigor that have been such an influence through the perilous passages of this 20th century of ours. Volumes will be written on the worth and wit that sweetened the greetings and the meetings as men make contact with their priceless possession—the spoken word.

That hearty, happy voice is silent now. His mortality has found its journey's end and its journey's beginning. The magnolia-shaded spot is almost within arm's reach of the crossroads where the boy split fence rails to earn his education. He sleeps in the Kentucky earth of his boyhood—restfully, rightfully, forever—his home.

No man could compress into one volume or one speech the wealth of these 78 years of living for and giving to mankind.

And let no man dare to say that "finis" has been written to ALBEN BARKLEY's creed or deeds.

For they will survive and serve as long as we cherish our heritage from him—we who have been his beneficiaries; we who share the continuity of the responsibilities he has laid down.

His ideas will survive and serve as long as we, in our consciousness and conscience, are true to his example—his fellow servants in the house of the Lord God of hosts, guide and guardian of the destinies of our beloved land.

WEDNESDAY, *May 9, 1956.*

Mr. FULBRIGHT. Mr. President, as were all other Members of the Senate, I was deeply shocked by the death of the beloved Senator from Kentucky, ALBEN BARKLEY. His passing marks the end of one of the great statesmen of our time. Although I shall miss his personal counsel and his great leadership, I am grateful for having had the opportunity of serving in the Senate with such a fine man.

Shortly after news of Senator BARKLEY's death was flashed over the radio, Mr. Edward R. Murrow gave his nightly comment on the news over the Columbia Broadcasting System.

His tribute to Senator BARKLEY expresses better than anything I can say the sense of loss which all of us felt so deeply. I ask unanimous consent to have printed at this point in the Record an excerpt from Mr. Murrow's commentary.

There being no objection, the excerpt from the commentary was ordered to be printed in the Record, as follows:

In the woods, when a great and ancient tree that has weathered many storms suddenly comes crashing down, there is the noise of smaller trees snapping back into position, the rustle and cries of small creatures, and the descending noise of twigs, branches, and bits of moss falling to the ground. And then there is silence, more complete and oppressive than any silence that went before. Frequently this happens on a dead calm day, for no apparent reason. So it was today with Senator ALBEN BARKLEY, of Kentucky. He was making the keynote speech at Washington and Lee University. The occasion was their mock democratic convention. The Senator had just said: "I would rather be a servant in the House of the Lord than sit in the seats of the mighty." He collapsed and was pronounced dead 10 minutes later.

It was altogether typical of the man that he devoted his last hour to politics and to youth. He was a man without cant, without rancor; a politician respected and admired, even by his opponents. In defeat he was resolute, and in victory indeed magnanimous. Few men have ever so endeared themselves in the hearts of their fellow men. He had humor, but seldom used it to hurt. He was a man who wore both power and popularity loosely, almost carelessly, like an old cloak. He was tolerant of most things, except intolerance. He had been in politics since 1905. He was helpful to young men. He was a tireless political campaigner. And he was an orator of what is generally called "the old school." Anyone who heard his keynote speech in Philadelphia in 1948, or his brilliant performance at Chicago in 1952, heard political oratory at its best. At Chicago he had thought the presidential nomination to be within his grasp. He lost it, knew he had lost it, and then went before the convention, shrugged his broad shoulders and proceeded to demonstrate how a good politician and a good loser should act and speak.

He served as Vice President under Mr. Truman, became known as the Veep, and was always the gentleman from Paducah. He loved the cut and thrust of parliamentary debate. He was known during his years in the Senate as the ready man, ready at the drop of a gavel to deliver a brilliant and lengthy speech, without benefit of notes or ghostwriters. While he was Vice President he refused to have a bodyguard, saying: "I'm a big boy now, and who would want to harm a young man like me, anyway?"

He was loyal to his party, but did not hesitate to break with Roosevelt in 1944 when the President vetoed a tax bill.

He was a man with manners, who liked people, who enjoyed good stories, some of them were old, but they were reinvigorated by the BARKLEY telling. After he finished his term as Vice President, he spent a couple of years in Kentucky and then went back to politics. He was elected the State's junior Senator for the term beginning in January of last year. So he went back to Congress where he had first arrived as a Representative in 1913. He once said he hoped to keep on politicking to the end—and he did.

The tributes, the expressions of shock and sorrow, are already coming in. Senator Knowland, of California, says: "The country and Kentucky have lost a great citizen and a great Senator." Senator Lehman, of New York, says: "Senator BARKLEY's death is a great shock to me, and a national disaster. His place in history is secure, but his place in our hearts will never be filled." McClellan, of Arkansas: "The Nation has lost a great man; one of the most beloved men in America." Ellender, of Louisiana: "He was a great American and a great statesman. We have suffered a very grievous loss." Former President Truman called him a citizen that the United States can always be proud of. President Eisenhower said: "The Nation is the poorer by this tragic event."

To this reporter Senator BARKLEY was always a man who took his duties and his responsibilities seriously, but who was always able to laugh, both at himself and his opposition. There will be many tributes to his ability, his loyalty, and his humor. Some of them will be eloquent. But mostly they will resemble the sound of smaller trees snapping upright, branches, twigs, and moss falling to the ground—after a giant tree has come crashing down.

WEDNESDAY, *May 16, 1956.*

Mr. SPARKMAN. Mr. President, I ask unanimous consent to have printed in the Record a poem written by Mr. Horace C. Carlisle, who now lives at Winston-Salem, N. C., but who was formerly a resident of Alabama, in tribute to our late beloved colleague, Senator BARKLEY.

There being no objection, the poem was ordered to be printed in the Record, as follows:

HUMANITY'S LOSS

S-enator Barkley, great statesman, is dead—
E-very man's friend and no mortal man's foe,
N-ational leader, of no one afraid,
A-s he fought wrong, in high places and low.
T-rue to his Nation, his State, and his own,
O-nward and upward, he kept keeping on,
R-elaxing not 'til his time came to go.

B-ravely contending for justice and right,
A-s he concluded his last speech, he fell—
R-eally he died without fear or affright,
K-nowing, beyond a doubt, that all was well.
L-ong in our memory will live his name—
E-very year will, methinks, add to his fame—
Y-onder in glory he's gone home to dwell.

—*Horace C. Carlisle.*

WEDNESDAY, *May 16, 1956.*

Mr. CLEMENTS. Mr. President, I ask unanimous consent to have printed in the Record, and appropriately referred, a resolution adopted by the board of directors of the Burley Tobacco Growers Cooperative Association, Inc., expressing appreciation of the splendid efforts of the late Senator ALBEN W. BARKLEY, of Kentucky, in behalf of agriculture.

There being no objection, the resolution was ordered to lie on the table, and to be printed in the Record, as follows:

RESOLUTION OF BURLEY TOBACCO GROWERS COOPERATIVE ASSOCIATION

The death of Senator ALBEN W. BARKLEY brought to an end a career of 50 years in public office marked by his effective championship of the proper application by Government of the principles of the democratic philosophy to the problems and concerns of common people and by his recognized superior leadership in the councils of his party and of his country.

A better and happier existence for all engaged in the basic industry of agriculture was one of the dominating desires of his life and particularly in the field of tobacco did he contribute his most vigorous and effective work to that end. Raised in the "tobacco patch" and for that reason acquainted at first hand with the adversities and hardships of tobacco growing, the plight and plea of the tobacco farmer always aroused sympathetic response in the mind and heart of the man who was regarded by so many as the Nation's greatest legislator. To ALBEN W. BARKLEY much credit is due for the legislative reforms and programs which have brought to the tobacco growers of the Nation stability of income which contributes measureably to the better and happier life for them which he desired and worked for throughout his whole career. His like will not soon succeed to the large role his death vacates. Therefore be it

Resolved by the board of directors of the Burley Tobacco Growers Cooperative Association of Lexington, Ky., That in the passing of ALBEN W. BARKLEY, the tobacco growers of Kentucky and of the Nation have lost a friendly and effective champion of their cause in the Congress but his great efforts in the half century of public service will continue in the future to yield untold profits and benefits to all who engage in growing tobacco.

It is ordered that a copy of this resolution be entered upon the permanent records of the association and a copy be sent to the family of Senator BARKLEY.

> JOHN JONES,
> JOHN M. BERRY,
> W. L. STATON,
> *Executive Committee.*

WEDNESDAY, *May 16, 1956.*

Mr. JOHNSON of Texas. Mr. President, I ask unanimous consent that the Senate proceed to the consideration of Calendar No. 2012, Senate Joint Resolution 166, and I call the attention of the distinguished Senator from Kentucky [Mr. Clements] to the request.

The PRESIDING OFFICER. The joint resolution will be stated by title for the information of the Senate.

The LEGISLATIVE CLERK. A joint resolution (S. J. Res. 166) to designate the dam and reservoir to be constructed on the lower Cumberland River, Kentucky, as Barkley Dam and Lake Barkley, respectively.

The PRESIDING OFFICER. Is there objection to the unanimous consent request of the Senator from Texas?

There being no objection, the Senate proceeded to consider the joint resolution.

Mr. CLEMENTS. Mr. President, the purpose of the joint resolution is to designate the lower Cumberland lock and dam on the Cumberland River, Ky., and the reservoir created thereby, as the Barkley Dam and Lake Barkley, respectively, in honor of the late Senator and former Vice President of the United States, ALBEN W. BARKLEY.

The site of the proposed lower Cumberland lock and dam is on the Cumberland River in Lyon and Livingston Counties, Ky., 30.5 miles above the confluence of the Cumberland and Ohio Rivers.

The project was authorized by Public Law 780, 83d Congress, in accordance with the recommendations contained in Senate Document No. 81, 83d Congress. The project is a multiple-purpose development for navigation, flood control, hydroelectric power, and other purposes. The reservoir will have a total capacity of 3,248,000 acre-feet, and a power installation of 130,000 kilowatts. The reservoir will extend about 120 miles upstream, a portion being in Tennessee, and have an area of approximately 100,000 acres. The estimated cost of the project is $167 million, and initiation of construction thereon is anticipated in the near future. The dam site is only a few miles from the Kentucky Dam, and the reservoir will extend almost parallel to Kentucky Lake, the largest reservoir of the Tennessee Valley Authority.

The lower Cumberland lock and dam project is located in the district in Kentucky in which the late Senator ALBEN W. BARKLEY resided. He was always a strong advocate and supporter of this project.

The committee believes it fitting and proper that this dam and reservoir bear the name of Barkley Dam and Lake Barkley in honor of the great statesman and beloved American from Kentucky, who so ably served his State and the Nation in public office for over 50 years. The committee realizes that no engineering structure is capable of symbolizing the greatness of the man ALBEN W. BARKLEY, but we can honor his life in a modest manner by having this dam and reservoir bear his name.

The PRESIDING OFFICER. The question is on the engrossment and third reading of the joint resolution.

The joint resolution (S. J. Res. 166) was ordered to be engrossed for a third reading, read the third time, and passed, as follows:

Resolved, etc., That the dam to be constructed on the lower Cumberland River, Ky., authorized by the Flood Control Act of 1954, and the reservoir to be formed by the waters impounded by such dam, shall hereafter be known as Barkley Dam and Lake Barkley, respectively, and any law, regulation, document, or record of the United States in which such dam and reservoir are designated or referred to shall be held to refer to such dam and reservoir under and by the names Barkley Dam and Lake Barkley, respectively.

The preamble was agreed to.

THURSDAY, May 17, 1956.

Mr. CLEMENTS. Mr. President, I ask unanimous consent to have printed in the body of the Record a beautfiul tribute which the Honorable Scott W. Lucas has written in memory of our beloved mutual friend and distinguished colleague, the late Honorable ALBEN W. BARKLEY.

There being no objection, the tribute was ordered to be printed in the Record, as follows:

SENATOR ALBEN BARKLEY

In the evening of life a great and good American, yea, the No. 1 voice of the Democratic Party, is silenced by the hand of death.

The once vibrant and gracious Veep has vanished, leaving the mortal flesh to sleep peacefully throughout the years of eternity.

In this fateful hour there are no ceremonies of pomp and splendor; all is still, save the mournful organ and the minister's moving voice.

So, the journey to the grave begins, moving across plains, mountains, and cities, midst the people he loved and who loved him.

And, at the journey's end, his everlasting place of rest is found in Kentucky soil—soil that made him—soil that he worshiped.

This noble and patriotic character leaves behind a record for God and country that has few parallels in American history.

God grant that more Barkleys may spring from Kentucky soil. Such men in American life are indispensable if the destinies of humanity are to remain free.

MONDAY, *June 18, 1956.*

The PRESIDENT pro tempore laid before the Senate the following resolution adopted by the Senate of the Republic of the Philippines, which was read, and ordered to lie on the table:

Whereas press dispatches have brought the shocking report of the sudden death of Senator ALBEN W. BARKLEY of the United States Congress; and

Whereas, as former Vice President and Senator before and at the time of his demise, ALBEN W. BARKLEY was a great friend of the Filipinos and contributed much to harmonious Philippine-American relations: Now, therefore, be it

Resolved, To request and authorize the President of the Senate of the Philippines to transmit a message of sincerest sympathy and condolence of this legislative body for the untimely death of Senator ALBEN W. BARKLEY to the Senate of the United States, as well as to his beloved family.

TUESDAY, *June 5, 1956.*

Mr. FREAR. Mr. President, the Democratic Party and the Democratic League of the State of Delaware recently adopted, in assembly, memorial resolutions expressing profound sorrow over the death of one of our most beloved colleagues, the late ALBEN W. BARKLEY.

I ask unanimous consent to have these resolutions printed in the Record.

There being no objection, the resolutions were ordered to be printed in the Record, as follows:

RESOLUTIONS OF RESPECT ON THE DEATH OF THE HONORABLE ALBEN W.
BARKLEY

Whereas the Lord God Almighty in His infinite wisdom and mercy has seen fit to call to Himself from this mortal world our

beloved associate and leader, ALBEN W. BARKLEY, a great and devoted and dedicated Christian servant; and

Whereas he was our warm friend, our inspired leader, and a
faithful public servant of the people of the United States; and

Whereas our hearts are full of sadness and grief for the great
loss which we the people of Delaware share with his widow, his
family, and the people of the Nation: Now, therefore, be it

Resolved, That we, the Democratic Party of Delaware in convention in Dover, Del., this day, do sincerely and reverently express our deep sympathy to the widow of our former Vice President
of the United States; and be it further

Resolved, That copies of this resolution be delivered to our
United States Senator, J. Allen Frear, Jr., and our United States
Congressman, Harris B. McDowell, Jr., requesting them to spread
it upon the pages of the Congressional Record in token of the
esteem and affection of the people of Delaware for our former Vice
President and friend.

Sincerely and sympathetically,

GARRETT E. LYONS,
State Chairman.
MARY B. CAHALAN,
Secretary.

Drawn as directed in convention at Dover, Del., May 25, 1956.

MEMORIAL

At the regular meeting of the Democratic League of Delaware,
held Monday, April 30, 1956, the following resolutions were unanimously adopted:

"*Resolved,* That as members of the Democratic League of Delaware, we record this expression of our sorrow at the death on
Monday, April 30, 1956, of our fellow member, ALBEN W. BARKLEY.

"His long and unselfish service both to the Government of the
United States and to the Democratic Party made him known, respected, and loved by all who hold dear the finest traditions of
our American way of life. His vigorous and tireless efforts to further these traditions will ever live as one of the outstanding
glories of the democratic ideal. Though we have lost his sparkling
companionship and though his eloquent voice is now forever stilled,
yet shall his memory live in our hearts as the symbol of the best
of American initiative, political courage, and moral force.

"*Resolved,* That we extend to his family our most heartfelt sympathy in their bereavement, and that a copy of this memorial resolution be sent to them."

For the Democratic League of Delaware:

JOHN J. CLARKE,
President.

JOHN A. HULL,
W. R. STEWART, SR.,
HARRIS O. BUNEL,
FRANK T. DICKERSON,
Secretary.

Memorial Services

❧

The Chaplain, Rev. Frederick Brown Harris, D. D., offered the following prayer:

Blessed be Thy name, most gracious God and Father of mankind, Thou who once again hath brought light out of darkness and, opening the gates of the morning, dost send us forth with powers of mind and body to front the duties and responsibilities of another day and another week. Go with us, we beseech Thee, through all the toiling, sunlit hours, and so protect us from every evil way that when evening comes we may have no stain of shame on our record. To this end give us this day the grace of a grateful heart and uncomplaining spirit—the grace of courage to stand for what our conscience tells us is the right; the grace of silence that we may refrain from unkind speech; the grace of charity that we may not give way to hasty judgment; the grace of refusing to conform rather than to crucify our convictions; and, in all, the calm confidence that—

> We steadier step
> When we recall
> That though we slip
> Thou dost not fall.

We ask it in the name of that One who is able to keep us from falling and to lead us on from strength to strength. Amen.

Mr. CLEMENTS. Mr. President, I send to the desk a resolution with reference to the death of the late Senator BARKLEY, which I ask to have stated and considered.

[73]

The resolution (S. Res. 308) was read, considered by unanimous consent, and unanimously agreed to, as follows:

Resolved, That the legislative business of the Senate be now suspended in order that memorial addresses may be delivered on the life, character, and public service of Hon. ALBEN W. BARKLEY, formerly Vice President of the United States, and late a Senator from the State of Kentucky.

Mr. CLEMENTS. Mr. President, on May 7 of this year a number of Members of the Senate expressed their sentiments upon the loss of a great American, a very distinguished son of Kentucky, ALBEN W. BARKLEY. On that occasion I expressed my own sentiments with respect to this great son of Kentucky. Today I should like to add briefly to those expressions.

Throughout his life Senator ALBEN W. BARKLEY was a man who always valued the deed higher than the word. To this great man, master of the spoken word though he was, actions—affirmative actions—always spoke louder than words.

His life was a life of action and his actions were taken in the name of democracy. He believed "What was good for the greatest number of people was best for the whole people."

Today, as we, his colleagues, honor his memory, I am proud that we in this Chamber and in this Congress have honored him with an affirmative action. By designating that the multipurpose dam on the lower Cumberland River near Kuttawa shall be called Barkley Dam, and that the reservoir created by this dam shall be called Lake Barkley, we have provided our beloved colleague with a living memorial.

Throughout his unparalleled career, Senator BARKLEY had a profound interest in this project. Every Kentuckian familiar with his lifelong devotion to the development of Kentucky's waterways, will realize, as I do, how much this gesture would have meant to our favorite son. I am glad the Congress appropriated the funds to commence this great project, for this was action which speaks more loudly than words ever could of the esteem we felt for him.

[74]

I will always count it as one of the great privileges of my life that I had the opportunity to work closely with Senator BARKLEY during the last year and a half of his life, following his return to the Senate in 1955. Our discussions about the problems of Kentucky and of the Nation, both on and off the floor, were frequent. It was my privilege to be closely associated with him since the time he first made a statewide race in Kentucky in the year 1923.

Though time has passed, our sense of loss at Senator BARKLEY's passing has not lessened. We here today can take comfort in the fact that though the body of a man may perish his work lives on.

As Representative, Senator, and Vice President he helped clear the frontiers of an adult America—frontiers dark with economic, social, and humanitarian problems. He was one of those who made our recent past a Golden Age in American development. Between 1937 and 1947, he was the majority leader of this great body, and guided into being much of the great legislation of that historic decade. Following the war his powerful, tireless voice was raised in a call for responsibility and America met her responsibilities as a great world power.

Yes, Mr. President, the work of ALBEN BARKLEY lives on.

Today, as on the day when this great man fell—a prayer on his lips—I find some comfort in the thought that the last sound ALBEN BARKLEY heard was the sound of the American people applauding. The young Americans attending a student political convention in Lexington, Va., has just applauded his words when he fell. The sound of their applause still hung in the air, and I like to think that the applause of the American people, which he deserved so well, was the sound that ALBEN BARKLEY carried with him into eternity.

None of us will ever forget his deeds. None will ever forget his last words:

I would rather be a servant in the House of the Lord than sit in the seats of the mighty.

Mr. President, under date of June 27, 1956, the supreme lodge of B'nai B'rith addressed to me the following letter:

B'NAI B'RITH,
Washington, D. C., June 27, 1056.

Hon. EARLE C. CLEMENTS,
United States Senate, Washington, D. C.

DEAR SENATOR CLEMENTS: It is with a deep sense of solemn gratification that I enclose a copy of a resolution passed by the supreme lodge of B'nai B'rith at its 21st general convention held in Washington, D. C., May 5–9, 1956.

As you will note, the resolution has been commended to you for presentation to the United States Senate, and it is respectfully requested that you do so.

Sincerely,

MAURICE BISGYER,
Executive Vice President.

Mr. President, the resolution relating to ALBEN W. BARKLEY, adopted at the 21st general convention of the supreme lodge of B'nai B'rith on May 5–9, 1956, is as follows:

RESOLUTION ON ALBEN W. BARKLEY

(Passed at 21st general convention of supreme lodge of B'nai B'rith, May 5–9, 1956)

On April 30, 1956, America lost one of its most beloved sons. ALBEN W. BARKLEY, in a long life filled with solid achievements, attained greatness as an American, as a statesman, as a humanitarian, and—as important as any of these—as a man.

His sense of dedication to his country and mankind was manifested from the beginning of his career to his awe-inspiring last words:

"I would rather be a servant of the Lord than sit in the seats of the mighty."

It was given to him to do both.

He never failed to answer the call of service. Even at the height of his career, when he was Vice President of the United States, and later, when he was the acknowledged dean of the Senate, he responded to such calls with typical energy, imagination, and the sparkling wit that characterized his lovable personality. He aided innumerable good causes, among them agencies of prime importance to the welfare of the Jewish people, here and abroad.

We of B'nai B'rith will never forget the inspiring address he delivered to our supreme lodge convention of 1950, here in the

Nation's Capital. In it he expressed his special pride in B'nai B'rith because it "sought to break down the barriers of bigotry and intolerance and hatred, and teach the brotherhood of man." He also hailed the order because it helped teach Americans of different backgrounds, religions, and economic and political status that they could "live together as neighbors and as friends and as Americans."

That was the kind of human being ALBEN BARKLEY was himself. His like will not soon be found again. Of him we say, as we do of our own Jewish sages, "His memory will be for a blessing."

It is directed that a copy of this resolution be sent to Mrs. Alben W. Barkley and to Senator Earle C. Clements for presentation to the Senate of the United States.

Mr. HUMPHREYS of Kentucky. Mr. President, I probably knew ALBEN BARKLEY over a longer period of time than did any of the other Members of this body. I knew him long before I was old enough to vote, in 1912. I was active in his campaign, and in getting the voters to the polls when he first ran for Congress. Although today, for a few brief weeks, I sit in his seat, no one can fill it. For a few very brief weeks I occupy his seat until someone more worthy can be elected.

I pay tribute today to ALBEN W. BARKLEY as the greatest citizen and man I have been privileged to know during my lifetime. All the Nation mourns his passing. We pay tribute to his magnificent leadership, and the fine influence he had on his State and Nation. I testify to his great service.

Mr. HILL. Mr. President, ALBEN BARKLEY in his autobiography, That Reminds Me, written some 3 years ago, declared:

Looking back on my three-quarters of a century—47 years of which have been spent in public service—I am bound to say it has been a good life. A good life and a full one. I have had my moments of sorrow and disappointment, as have all who are born on this earth, but there has been no prolonged period when I have not found life filled with joy and zest. I have been proud, too, of the opportunities given me to serve my country.

It was in an hour of joy and zeal that ALBEN BARKLEY passed out of the company of living men, for nothing pleased him more than to stand before his fellow men, to speak to them, to illustrate with his inimitable stories, to expound the gospel of the Democratic Party which he loved so well, and to proclaim the faith by which he lived. We know how powerful, how persuasive, how compelling was his logic and his eloquence, how withering his sarcasm, how devastating his wit, all combining to make him the Nation's foremost political orator. Who that heard him can ever forget his memorable speech in the late evening at the Philadelphia 1948 Democratic Convention that lifted the discouraged and disheartened delegates, moved and inspired them, and sent them forth with fire in their eyes and resolution in their hearts to win the victory? After the speech there was no longer any question as to who the nominee of the convention for Vice President would be. All eyes and all hands had turned to ALBEN BARKLEY.

Proud of the opportunities given to him to serve his country, he met them, he gloriously measured up to them—from log cabin, county prosecutor, county judge, Congressman, Senator, to Vice President. Vice Presidents have come and gone, many of them, but we have had only one so outstanding in personality, in leadership and in service to our country, and so strong in the appreciation and affections of the American people as to become "Mr. Veep." Like that other immortal Kentuckian, Henry Clay, his name and fame outshone even many of those who have held the great office of President of the United States.

ALBEN BARKLEY was majority leader of the Senate longer than any man in American history. It was my honor and privilege to be his assistant as Democratic whip of the Senate for 6 years. He tells us in his autobiography that in the extremely close contest between him and another great American, the late Pat Harrison, of Mississippi, when he was first elected majority leader, he solicited no votes. ALBEN

BARKLEY did not solicit votes. He led men by the example of his life, the influence of his character, his courage, his devotion to principles and his steadfast adherence to his convictions, and by his masterful and eloquent presentation of the issues. ALBEN BARKLEY led men by the force of his genius. And if he lost he never complained, and his sense of justice and of the eternal fitness of things never failed him. There was no vanity in him. There was no retribution in his spirit. There was no littleness in the man. There was so tempered in the heart and soul of ALBEN BARKLEY elements of tolerence, patience, and sympathy that he drew to him the ungrudging regard and affection of all men who came within the radius of his genial influence.

In his autobiography he refers to the honors that were accorded him, and then he declares:

If I had to choose the phrasing of any particular commendation as words that I would like to be remembered by, I think I might lean toward the citation which accompanied the Collier's award, which I received in May 1948. In naming me as the outstanding Senator during the previous year, when the opposition party was in power and I had stepped down from majority to minority leader, the awards committee was quoted as saying:

"Under conditions that would have caused a less determined man to walk out and rest, he continued to work for his country through the party. * * * His good temper was as always a good influence in the Senate. * * * His ability in rough and ready debate, his remarkable capacity to argue powerfully on many and diverse issues, and his acceptance of demotion without a trace of venom, made him the Grand Old Man of the Senate last year. As his position came down he seemed to grow in stature."

Is it surprising that the last words to fall from the lips of such a man were, "I would rather be a servant in the house of the Lord than sit in the seat of the mighty"? We know that ALBEN BARKLEY served nobly and well in the house of the Lord.

We shall ever miss ALBEN BARKLEY. We shall ever miss the laughter of his rich humor, and inimitable stories, the sunshine and warmth of his friendship, the joy of his companionship, the gold of his wisdom, and the inspiration of his leadership.

ALBEN BARKLEY as a young man attended for a short period Thomas Jefferson's university, the University of Virginia. There he breathed deep the air of Jefferson's philosophy, found and nurtured his spiritual kinship with the immortal author of the Declaration of Independence, and was ever the disciple and prophet of Jeffersonian democracy. He recognized that great forces were loose in America and that great changes were taking place. He knew that when a nation grows rich and powerful it can become careless and forget its ideals.

ALBEN BARKLEY labored and fought for the preservation and the perfecting of American democracy. He fought against special privilege, monopoly, the mastery of the many by the few. He fought to open wide the door of economic opportunity, to redress social wrongs, to correct political abuses. He was on the side of the underprivileged, the less fortunate, the little folks. He was the champion of the people and a mighty warrior for peace for ourselves and for all nations. In the closing words of his autobiography he declares:

I believe there are certain things which are still crying for accomplishment in this country. I shall continue to raise my voice for them.

And then he concludes:

I should like to live to see every American family living in a comfortable home, and every American child born and reared in an atmosphere sufficiently wholesome to guarantee an even chance for health and intellectual and moral development consonant with the responsibilities of American citizenship. I should like to live to see the world at peace, where the inventive genius of man would be utilized to improve the conditions of life throughout the world. I should like to live to see the pledge of every nation respected by every other nation because it was made in good faith and observed to the letter.

So long as America shall stand in history, the example of the life and character and services of ALBEN BARKLEY will be remembered—will challenge and inspire men and women to carry on and fight on for the ideals and the principles that have made our America great. As was said of that other native son of Kentucky, that towering figure and great American, Abraham Lincoln, it may be said of ALBEN BARKLEY:

> He held his place—
> Held the long purpose like a growing tree
> Held on though blame and faltered not at praise
> And when he fell in whirlwind, he went down
> As when a lordly cedar, green with boughs,
> Goes down with a great shout upon the hills
> And leaves a lonesome place against the sky.

Mr. EASTLAND. Mr. President, the State of Kentucky has given to this Nation many great and illustrious sons to serve in the Halls of Congress and high positions of Government. No jewel in this State diadem of honor and devotion shines brighter than the one bearing the name ALBEN WILLIAM BARKLEY. From his earliest youth, Senator BARKLEY dedicated himself to a career of public service that extended over a period of more than 50 years as a lawyer, a prosecuting attorney, a judge, a Member of the United States House of Representatives, United States Senator, and Vice President of this country. He more than fulfilled the tasks assigned to him and grew each day in stature and understanding.

ALBEN BARKLEY was a man of the people and never lost that gracious and humane quality that made both loving and loved. His wit, humor, and human understanding were of a character that had never been equalled in contemporary time.

When duty called, ALBEN could always be counted on as the first to answer the summons. His fine and capable hands played a great and important part in the piloting of the State through the travail of the great economic depression that beset us, and, later, through two wars of awe-inspiring proportion.

ALBEN's sense of honor and duty were so deeply ingrained that he always asked himself but one question, "What course of action should I adopt consistent with the interests and needs of the people of this country?" When his course was set on this standard he was an immovable rock, impervious to the stresses and strains of expediency.

In the long history of this Senate few Members have ever been called upon to serve in more different and responsible positions than has he. As majority leader through the entire period of World War II, he bore responsibilities almost comparable to those of the President himself. It was most fitting and proper that he should have been promoted to the Vice Presidency and there also he acquitted himself in the same superlative fashion throughout another critical period in our history. No man ever received a more hearty "Welcome back" than did ALBEN when he returned to the Senate.

Mr. President, I say this with all the sincerity of my heart— that I do not know of any man who was ever more loved and respected by his colleagues in this body than was ALBEN BARKLEY. Neither time nor new faces can ever replace the void that is left by his passing. He was a giant among men and I know that if he had been permitted to dictate to the all-powerful Creator the time and moment of his passing he would not have chosen a course different from that which his life took; a worker in the vineyard, active and diligent to the very end.

Mr. SMITH of New Jersey. Mr. President, it was with profound sorrow that we all heard on April 30 of the sudden passing of our beloved colleague, ALBEN BARKLEY. All during the 12 years I have been a Member of the Senate I have looked upon ALBEN BARKLEY as one of my close friends. When those of us who came here in 1944 were freshmen it was ALBEN BARKLEY who was then majority leader, who offered a hand of warm welcome, and he was the first to give me that understanding and fellowship which is so strong here in the Senate between all of us on both sides of the aisle.

After being here a few years I had the great privilege of traveling with Senator BARKLEY in 1947 with a special senatorial committee to study the development of what came to be the USIA program. This is the so-called Smith-Mundt bill, which we all collaborated in developing and having passed in the Senate and House shortly after our return from that memorable trip. It was my privilege to get to know Senator BARKLEY well on that trip through the close contacts we had in our travels. In a number of places I had the good fortune to room with him when accommodations were scarce, and, of course, I had the high privilege of learning firsthand some of those wonderful anecdotes with which he always illustrated his thinking.

Since that time, of course, we had him with us as Vice President, and then last year he came back to us as a Member of the Senate after his vice presidential term had come to a close. Knowing ALBEN BARKLEY is one of those treasured recollections that come to us and will always remain with us.

He was one of the leaders of his party. He had great and vigorous talent in debate, and especially in summing up the administration's position when he was majority leader. He was unmatched by anyone in his good humor and his wit in illustrating his points with pertinent anecdotes.

Beyond all these qualities, however, we loved him for himself and for what his unfailing friendship meant to us as one of us.

Mrs. Smith and I extend to his wife and all the other members of his family our deepest sympathies and warm affections.

Mr. NEELY. Mr. President, in this Chamber on the 4th of March 1952 when Vice President BARKLEY was presiding, I attempted to pay him a tribute of esteem and love. Let me repeat what I then said as my contribution to this day's eulogies of this matchless and inimitable patriot, statesman, husband, father, and friend:

Mr. President, to endeavor to add anything of value to the glowing tributes, which have been most eloquently paid the greatest of all Vice Presidents in the Senate this afternoon, would be an undertaking as futile as an attempt—

"To paint the lily,
    Throw a perfume on the violet,
    Or add another color to the rainbow's gorgeous hues."

To eulogize Vice President BARKLEY, in accordance with his merits, is a task as impossible of performance as was that of the vestal virgin who, in order to prove her innocence, was required to carry water in a sieve from the banks of the Tiber to the top of the Capitoline Hill. Nevertheless it is impossible for me to resist the temptation to borrow a few expressions from certain immortals and, subject to slight change, utilize them in behalf of the preeminently useful, eloquent, and beloved ALBEN W. BARKLEY, who habitually dispenses justice in the Senate as Solomon administered it from his throne.

In anticipation and spirit, the world's greatest dramatist said of you, Mr. President, long ago, and one of your most devoted friends says of you and to you now:

"When, in disgrace with fortune and men's eyes,
    I all alone beweep my outcast state,
And trouble deaf Heaven with my bootless cries,
    And look upon myself, and curse my fate,
Wishing me like to one more rich in hope,
    Featured like him, like him with friends possess'd,
Desiring this man's art and that man's scope,
    With what I most enjoy contented least;
Yet in these thoughts myself almost despising,
    (President BARKLEY) Haply I think on thee, and then my state,
Like to the lark at break of day arising
    From sullen earth, sings hymns at Heaven's gate;
For they sweet love remember'd such wealth brings
    That then I scorn to change my state with kings."

Mr. President, you first came to the House of Representatives on the 4th of March 1913. As the result of a special election, it was my honor and privilege to become your colleague and gain your acquaintance in that great legislative Chamber on the first day of the following November. The warm friendship between us that then and there leaped into life has never, so far as I am concerned, lost a single trace of its vigor or a single scintilla of its value.

During the intervening years, by virtue of unsurpassable public service as a Congressman, a United States Senator, majority leader of the Senate, and Vice President of the United States, you have won international fame, bestowed deathless blessings upon humanity, and inscribed your name in the golden book of immortality. For your meticulous patriotism we extol you, for your matchless eloquence we laud you, for your unfailing humanitarian service we love you.

Kentucky—one of the Nation's most prolific progenitors of immortality—has given the world none nobler, greater, or grander than you. To the hosts who intimately know you and the millions who dearly love you, you are—

"A spring of ice-cold water to the parched and burning lips of
    thirst;
A palm that lifts its cornet of leaves above the desert sand;
An isle of green in some far sea;
The purple light of dawn above the eastern hills;
A cloud of gold beneath the setting sun;
A fragrance wafted from an unseen shore;
A silvery strain of music heard within some palace wrought of
    dreams."

Mr. President, we sincerely wish you very much longer life, perfect health, and unlimited success, prosperity, happiness, and peace. Our fond recollections of you and of the inspiration, the friendship, and the kindness with which you have infinitely enriched our lives will be to the end of our days:

"The rainbow to our storms of life,
    The evening beam that smiles the clouds away,
    And tints tomorrow with prophetic ray."

Mr. JOHNSTON of South Carolina. Mr. President, a man I loved—the great warrior and servant of the people—has died.

The void that is left in our lives, in this Chamber, and in the Democratic Party will never again be adequately filled. The great ALBEN BARKLEY will never be replaced, for when God makes men such as he they live only once.

But we who knew ALBEN BARKLEY, and those of this generation who write history, know that ALBEN BARKLEY will never be forgotten. His imprint upon the history of America will be here for as long as this Nation survives.

When I was returning to Washington on the train the day he died, a hundred images of ALBEN BARKLEY passed through my mind. I saw him as the tireless warrior of the people who spent his adult lifetime fighting for the principles that serve the common everyday people of this great land. I saw him as the champion of the democratic people of this Nation. When any battle of the Democratic Party seemed faltering, whether it was in my native State of South Carolina or in some farflung corner of the land, without fail "Dear ALBEN" answered the call for help.

I saw ALBEN BARKLEY as the true Kentucky southern gentleman that he was—always as kindly and as neighborly to a stranger as he would be to the mightiest of the world. I remember well when in 1952 he came to aid the Democratic Party in South Carolina with his eloquent command of the English language. Many a farmer and many a cotton mill worker came up to shake his hand. With the same warmth and fervor he would use to greet his colleagues in the United States Senate, ALBEN BARKLEY, the Vice President, met my people.

I saw ALBEN BARKLEY, too, as he delivered his last nationwide address at the Woodrow Wilson testimonial dinner in Washington. I saw his upraised hands, I heard his strong voice, his determined diction, his logical reasoning—and, yes, I saw his trademark, the flinching of his shoulders to adjust his coat—as he paid tribute to the great figures of the Democratic Party of the past half century.

Perhaps I should not mention partisanship at a time like this; but ALBEN BARKLEY was a partisan man as well as a statesman. He believed in the Democratic Party, he fought for the democratic processes, and he died fighting for the same causes with unsurpassed loyalty and devotion. Certainly no man of partisanship in our generation was ever admired, loved, and held in such great esteem by men of all parties as was ALBEN BARKLEY. This, alone, is a tribute to this man's greatness.

As we well know, with all his partisanship, ALBEN BARKLEY never once faltered in determining first that whatever he decided to fight for would be in the best interest of this Nation which he loved above all else. By human custom we are politicians today, and statesmen only in the retrospect of those who survive us. But I believe ALBEN BARKLEY was judged a statesman by people everywhere, long before anyone conceived of his passing.

Mr. President, the mightiest of the oaks of the forest has fallen. A giant among the characters of this generation has departed. Certainly nothing that any of us can say will adequately testify to what stirs within us when we think of the death of ALBEN BARKLEY.

As in all things, we must go on. Our Nation will continue to progress. We will continue in our search for perpetual peace and freedom for this world. But none of us—no, not one—will go on in these endeavors without having first benefited because ALBEN BARKLEY lived. As we go forward together, ALBEN BARKLEY shall continue to live through us and those that succeed us by the things he said, taught, and did when he was among us.

It is ironic, but no testimony from anyone on earth could more competently describe the life of ALBEN BARKLEY than the very last words which he, himself, uttered as he left us to join God:

I would rather be a servant in the House of the Lord than to sit in the seats of the mighty.

Mr. LEHMAN. Mr. President, with the untimely passing of ALBEN W. BARKLEY the Congress of the United States lost one of its most distinguished and most beloved Members and the Nation lost one of its greatest sons. The Veep was an extraordinary man—kindly, wise, and experienced beyond most men, and ever devoted to the interests of his country, without regard to partisanship. He had the unique ability to inspire and move his fellow citizens to action, and to reflect their views and their high ideals.

I was honored by his friendship long before I came to the Senate. There was no man in public life for whom I had greater admiration and affection. He was unquestionably one of the greatest men of our times. Few men have equaled his record of useful achievement and service. I know of no man living today who has excelled that splendid record. I shall always be thankful that I had the opportunity of serving with him for nearly 7 years in this great body and of observing and benefiting from his wise counsel, his forbearance, and his unending patience.

We in the Senate have greatly missed him as a great leader whose place in history is assured. Above all things, however, we miss him and shall continue to miss him as a beloved friend who had earned and held our respect and our deep love. ALBEN BARKLEY will never be forgotten.

Mr. JOHNSON of Texas. Mr. President, every once in awhile as we travel the highways of life, we meet a man who sums up in his own character the heart and the soul of a whole nation.

Such a person was our dearly beloved colleague, the late ALBEN W. BARKLEY, of Kentucky.

There are many things that can be said about ALBEN BARKLEY, because his life was rich and full of meaning. They are things that have been said in the past and will be said again in the future, so long as historians concern themselves with this period of our history.

He was a wise man. He was a patriotic man. He was a courageous man. He was a man of conviction who dedicated his enormous talents to the service of our country.

The American people recognized these qualities, and they responded by awarding him high office and great trust. He sat in the highest councils of our land, and his words were heeded by chiefs of state throughout the world.

But he had one other quality which endeared him to our people and made his name a household word throughout our land. It was the quality of humanity—a rare blend of kindly humor and sympathetic understanding of his fellow mortals.

Americans everywhere looked upon his with an affection that was not only deep but personal. In households from his native Kentucky to the borders of our land he was regarded as a family friend that everyone hoped would soon drop in for a visit.

The years we spent with him were rewarding.

He had a genuine and unaffected interest in the problems of others. He was gentle—and it was the gentleness of a strong man who had no need to cover up weakness. He was witty—and it was a kindly wit that carried not a trace of malice.

As a result, people rejoiced with him when he was happy, mourned with him when he was sad. And at all times they reposed in him the trust and the confidence that are accorded only to very close and very dear friends.

He was known as the Veep, a nickname that summed up both the respect and the affection in which he was held. It was, in a very real sense, an accolade.

We shall miss ALBEN BARKLEY. There is no one who can quite take his place. We shall miss his warm humor and his gentle philosophy. We shall miss his wise counsel and prudent advice. We shall miss the zest with which he sallied forth to battle, and the equanimity with which he accepted victory or defeat.

But there is one consolation for his family and his friends. No one could know ALBEN BARKLEY without finding life a little better and a little more kindly.

And since his friends were practically all of our people, it can truly be said that he made this a better world.

Mr. HOLLAND. Mr. President, I am sure that the passing of Senator ALBEN W. BARKLEY, of Kentucky, brought sincere sorrow to every person who served with him in the United States Senate, both those who were here at the time of his death and that considerable number who were here during the earlier years of his service as a Senator and as Vice President. The Nation lost in Senator BARKLEY one of its most devoted and effective public servants, and one of the most colorful and best beloved public figures who has ever played an important part on the stage of American politics and government. Expressions of sincere admiration, unlimited confidence, and deep affection have come from people of all walks of life and in all parts of our Nation. I join wholeheartedly in those expressions, though I shall not attempt to reiterate or enlarge upon them.

I wish, however, to speak as one who attended Emory College, at Oxford, Ga., several years after Senator BARKLEY was a student there. Emory College, now Emory University, has for years regarded Senator BARKLEY as our most distinguished alumnus. His death brought expressions of high respect and affection from the student body, the faculty, the alumni, and the trustees.

Rather than attempt to make a statement of my own on behalf of Emory and sons of Emory, I shall read into the Record the article about him which appeared in the June 1956 issue of the Emory Alumnus. The title of the article is, "He Was a Servant in the House of the Lord," with this subtitle, "But ALBEN BARKLEY Also Sat in the Seats of the Mighty." I quote the article, as follows:

It already has been reported from one end of the world to the other that Emory's most famous and most widely loved alumnus, ALBEN WILLIAM BARKLEY, 1900–1949H, died on April 30 at the age of 78 while addressing students at Washington and Lee University, and that his last words were: "I would rather be a servant in the house of the Lord than sit in the seats of the mighty."

It already has been recorded thousands of times and thousands of places that Mr. BARKLEY has been: A Representative to Congress from the First Kentucky District in 1913–27; a Senator from his State in 1927–49, and in that period both majority leader and minority leader of that body; Vice President of the United States in 1949–53; "Mr. Democrat" himself, by virtue of being a delegate to every Democratic National Convention from 1920 on, a key figure in most of them and a man of unparalleled party loyalty; and junior Senator from 1955 to the time of his death.

These and many more things about the beloved "Veep" have been chronicled: The fact that he narrowly missed on at least one occasion being President of the United States; his oratorical ability; his wit and his story-telling prowess. It remains, then for his alma mater's magazine to give just a few facts about his connections with Emory:

Born in Lowes, Ky., Mr. BARKLEY entered Marvin College, a small institution in Mayfield, Ky., at the age of 14 and worked his way through, receiving an A. B. in 1897. To officials at Marvin—Mr. BARKLEY referred to them as copresidents—were Emory alumni, J. C. Speight and J. C. Dean, both of the class of 1886. On completing his work at Mayfield, Mr. BARKLEY decided to continue his formal education.

He selected Emory College, then located in Oxford, Ga., but later to become Emory University in Atlanta, "because it was one of the outstanding colleges in the country, because it was connected with one of the foremost churches, because it had graduated an impressive group of citizens—and because it had a loan fund."

Actually, the Veep-to-be spent only 1 academic year, 1897–98, at Emory. Since he entered as an advanced student in 1897, he was then and has since been classified as a member of the class of 1900. About 30 members of that class are still living, and their class councilman is Judge Jesse M. Wood, 1900, of Fulton superior court.

Mr. BARKLEY has since referred to Oxford as "this sacred old spot where I played and cantered as a boy and where I debated the great issues of the day." In one such debate, as a member of Few Literary Society debating Phi Gamma Literary Society, the man who was later to become the symbol of Democratic Party loyalty took the affirmative side of the question, "Resolved that independent action in politics is more desirable than party politics."

Years later he explained, "I convinced myself I was arguing the right side, but I soon learned better."

In his year at Old Emory, Mr. BARKLEY made 99 in punctuality, 100 in physical education, 95 in deportment, and between 85 and 95 in such subjects as geometry, Bible, Latin, Greek composition, trigonometry, geography, declamation, and English grammar. He won recognition for his speaking and debating talents, and was elected a member of Delta Tau Delta social fraternity. But he was not enrolled long enough to become a real campus leader. The student yearbook, the Zodiac, of 1898, even misspelled his first name by running it "ALLEN."

A profound and lasting impression on the Kentucky farm boy was made by Warren A. Candler, '75–'78H, who was then in the last year of his 10-year term as president of Emory. Throughout his later life Mr. BARKLEY quoted his Emory president. The two left Oxford at the same time, for President Candler was elevated to the Methodist episcopacy in the spring of 1898.

Mr. BARKLEY left Emory to study at the University of Virginia law school, read law in Paducah, Ky., practice law, and become a prosecuting attorney and judge before being elected to Congress for the first time. He visited Atlanta and Emory on several occasions thereafter, but the real visit was in June 1949, a few months after he had become Vice President.

On that occasion Vice President BARKLEY delivered the commencement address to the undergraduate divisions, was awarded the honorary doctor-of-laws degree, was initiated by the Emory chapter of Phi Beta Kappa, made an informal talk at Emory-at-Oxford, and spent a night as the guest of Emory president and Mrs. Goodrich C. White.

Emory's opinion of its best known alumnus was summed up by the politician who was asked if he liked Mr. BARKLEY:

"Anyone who doesn't like ALBEN BARKLEY," he said, "doesn't like the human race."

Mr. McCLELLAN. Mr. President, I can add very little to the very eloquent and fully deserved tributes which have been paid to our departed colleague, Senator BARKLEY, whom all of us loved. I wish to associate myself with all that has been said about him here this afternoon.

Mr. President, it was never my privilege or opportunity, since I have been a Member of the Senate, to serve on a committee with Senator BARKLEY. Quite often it is in the course of committee service, in working together, particularly in the consideration of highly controversial legislation, that one comes to know the real qualities of statesmanship his colleagues possess.

However, it has been my privilege, and one I shall always cherish, to serve with Senator BARKLEY in the United States Senate and to serve here when he was President of this body.

Senator BARKLEY will long be remembered, of course, for his marvelous achievements and his outstanding success in politics and in the affairs of state of our country. All those admirable accomplishments give him a place in history which will remain so long as our Nation survives.

In my associations and contacts with Senator BARKLEY, I knew him as one who was affable, friendly, kindly, and always considerate. I also knew him as one whose arguments and persuasion were forceful and convincing in debate.

Senator BARKLEY made a record of able and constructive service, one that will seldom be equalled by any other American statesman of our time or in the future.

Mr. President, these great qualities, and others of outstanding leadership, commanded the admiration and esteem of all the American people, regardless of political or partisan affiliation. Senator BARKLEY will be greatly missed.

I had a good many rather private conversations of a confidential nature with Senator BARKLEY.

Mr. President, my father, who now is 85 years old, and is retired, has long been a great admirer of Senator BARKLEY. My father's mind is still alert, and his interest in national affairs and national politics is just as keen as it ever has been. He frequently wrote to Senator BARKLEY.

I recall that one day after Senator BARKLEY became Vice President, and when he was presiding over the Senate, he sent a page to ask me to come to the rostrum. I did so, and there Senator BARKLEY showed me a letter he had received that day from my father, and he expressed his appreciation for the sentiments my father had written in the letter.

The day following Senator BARKLEY's passing, my father wrote me a letter in which he told of his deep sorrow and grief at the loss of this great statesman. In the course of the letter, he made many comments, and closed his references to Senator BARKLEY by expressing a sentiment which I think is shared by all Members of the Senate and by millions of other Americans all over the country. Therefore, Mr. President, I know of no better thought to express, no finer sentiment to voice at this moment, as I close these remarks, than the one my father stated in closing his letter to me:

His place in history is a bright spot on our Nation.

Mr. MARTIN of Pennsylvania. Mr. President, I join in the tributes to our great and beloved friend and colleague, ALBEN W. BARKLEY.

I shall always cherish the memory of my last meeting with Senator BARKLEY. It was on the Sunday before the Nation was plunged into sorrow by the tragic loss we have sustained in his untimely death. It was my privilege to be one of a group who chatted with Senator BARKLEY as the guests of Senator Byrd, on his Virginia farm. Senator BARKLEY's wonderful sense of humor and his sparkling wit made the occasion one which I shall always recall with fondest memories of a kindly, gracious, courteous gentleman who endeared himself to everyone who knew him.

Few men in public life have been so highly esteemed. Few men have held such a warm place in the affections of the whole Nation. His memory will be enshrined forever in the hearts of his fellow Americans.

With a profound sense of personal loss, I extend to his wife, his children, and his grandchildren my deepest sympathy in their bereavement.

Mr. HUMPHREY of Minnesota. Mr. President, I wish to join my colleagues in the Senate today with a few words of tribute in respect to our dearly beloved friend, the late Senator BARKLEY.

It is very difficult to find adequate or appropriate words to express one's heartfelt emotions concerning this magnifi-

cent man. Earlier in the proceedings of the Senate, immediately following the passing of Senator BARKLEY, I made a
few remarks which indicated the immediate feelings I had
over the loss of this dear friend and wonderful citizen.

Senator BARKLEY passed away as he was addressing a group
of young people at Washington and Lee University. This
was typical. He liked young people, because he was young
of spirit and young of mind. He saw in the young the hope
of the future. Senator BARKLEY always saw in young Americans an opportunity to interest young minds and hearts in
the welfare of their country. As a true patriot, he went to
that great source of patriotism, which is the enthusiastic
spirit and idealism of young men and women.

I think we shall always remember the parting words of our
late beloved friend, words which were so characteristic of
every aspect of his life. "I would rather be a servant in the
House of the Lord than to sit in the seats of the mighty."

ALBEN BARKLEY was a servant in the House of the Lord,
because he was the kind of man who was constantly doing
good. When I say that he was a good man, doing the work
of the Lord, I mean that Senator BARKLEY was kind to everyone; that he was considerate to people of different points of
view and different backgrounds; that he was always understanding; and that, above all, he was always helpful, willing
to assist others at all times.

If ever there was a man in public life who was a true
Christian and who practiced his religious ideals, it was ALBEN
BARKLEY. His religion was more than mere pronouncements.
It consisted in doing good work and good deeds for his fellow
men, recognizing at all times that God's greatest creation is
the individual created in the image of his Maker. It was to
the individual, his fellow man, that ALBEN BARKLEY dedicated his great resourcefulness, his fine talents, and his rare
ability.

The death of Senator BARKLEY was a shock to every American because he seemed almost indestructible. He surely

was indefatigable. He was always irrepressible. He was always constructive. I shall long remember and I am sure that the pages of history of our time will record—that ALBEN BARKLEY was a perpetual optimist. His optimism was not based upon fanciful thinking. Rather it was an optimism based upon a basic understanding of the strength and the great resourcefulness of the United States of America and its people.

We shall always miss Senator BARKLEY. We miss his words of counsel and advice. I am sure that those of us who are the younger Members of Congress will always remember the helpful advice and counsel which, upon request, was so generously given by this great American statesman. We shall miss his friendly words of encouragement. Senator BARKLEY seemed to have a propensity for understanding when his friends and colleagues needed a word of encouragement.

Above all, Mr. President, we miss his warm humor—not a synthetic humor, nor one created for the purpose of laughter alone, but rather a humor which arose from Senator BARKLEY'S understanding of the great life of the American Republic. It was always timely, and it was always meaningful; yet it was always refreshing and invigorating.

In his character, his demeanor, and his career, Senator ALBEN BARKLEY was truly representative of the United States of America. If any one man in our history ever really deserved the title of "Mr. America," it was the late Senator ALBEN BARKLEY. He rose from humble beginnings to positions of honor, respect, responsibility, and power; and in all his greatness he possessed a sense of humility and kindness which endeared him to everyone.

We know of his record as a Representative in Congress, as a United States Senator, as majority leader, and as Vice President of the United States, bringing new dignity and new responsibility to that great office. Then, Mr. President, he climaxed his career by returning to the Senate, this parliamentary body which he loved with every fiber of his being.

He came back to contribute from his great experience and wisdom to our deliberations and to the formulation of the policies of our Government.

I believe that above all ALBEN BARKLEY glorified the word "citizen." There is no greater title for a free man than citizen. ALBEN BARKLEY was a citizen in the fullest sense of the word. He was a participating citizen, active in the political life of his country.

He loved and honored his country by his works and by his words. He so loved and honored his home town of Paducah, Ky., that today every American upon hearing the name "Paducah" thinks of it as being the home of the Veep, the home of ALBEN BARKLEY. He surely loved and brought great fame to the great State of Kentucky.

He brought honor to the term "politician." Senator ALBEN BARKLEY was proud to be called a politician, because he saw in the term its true meaning, the science and study of government. ALBEN BARKLEY was a politician who had studied government and who knew government. He also knew that government in a free country was essentially the art and science of human relationships. He knew that for free government to be effective, it was necessary for those in positions of responsibility to have the ability to work together, cooperatively, and in that spirit ultimately to make decisions.

Senator BARKLEY was an impressive debater. He was able to muster all the facts for his argument and to base his cause upon sound logic, coupled with persuasive talents. He was one of the greatest orators of our century; indeed, he was one of the great political orators of all time.

Best of all, Mr. President, he was an advocate; be believed in things, and he made his beliefs and his conclusions crystal clear. He was willing to argue his case, without any bitterness or rancor or arrogance or intolerance.

Mr. President, our late beloved friend will always be remembered as a distinguished American statesman. But above all, in my mind, he will be remembered as a great statesman of the world, who made lasting contributions to human freedom which will bring to his name the fond remembrances of little people and of great people for centuries yet to come.

Mr. MURRAY. Mr. President, some weeks ago a Member of the Senate made a highly appropriate observation concerning the late Senator BARKLEY. He said Senator BARKLEY was the best-loved Member of the Senate.

Certainly no man ever endeared himself to his colleagues to a greater degree than the late Senator BARKLEY.

But ALBEN BARKLEY was more than the best-loved Member of this body. He was a great American and a friend of all mankind.

He had the high respect and admiration even of those with whom he disagreed. While he could devastate an opponent in debate he could also heal the wounds of controversy with the balm of his irrepressible good humor and boundless supply of delightful and appropriate stories.

Under the leadership of Senator BARKLEY, during his tenure as our majority leader, the Senate passed some of its most historic legislation of the Nation. During his term as Vice President of the United States he presided with skill and dignity over the deliberations of this body. Later he returned to the Senate determined to do all he could to carry forward the principles and programs he espoused. He passed on while doing one of the things he loved best, speaking to young Americans on his philosophy of government.

We have all lost a treasured friend. His memory shall be cherished by every American who had the privilege of knowing ALBEN BARKLEY. He has left his imprint on the Nation. His place in history is assured.

Mr. KEFAUVER. Mr. President, the passage of time has softened the shock we felt in company with other citizens throughout the Nation when we first learned of the death of Senator ALBEN BARKLEY.

Looking about this Chamber even today, however, I find it difficult to realize that he has irrevocably gone from us.

This body and the 48 States which it represents are poorer today for his absence.

ALBEN BARKLEY'S was a voice of sanity. He raised it often and well. He helped guide us through dark days which he brightened with the humor which reduced complicated issues to their basic essentials—expressed in warm and generous human terms. His loss is a loss to free men everywhere. He had no enemies. He hated only oppression, arrogance, and sham. He was ever a champion of the underprivileged and the depressed of no matter what creed or color or nationality.

ALBEN BARKLEY was not only a great American; he was a respected and loved citizen of the world. He was, indeed, as he said in his last statement "a servant of the Lord."

Although the place of ALBEN BARKLEY may be taken in this Chamber by good men, his place in our hearts, in our esteem, and in our memories can never be filled.

Mr. ROBERTSON. Mr. President, it would be futile for me to attempt to add to the tributes already paid to the outstanding accomplishments of our departed friend and colleague Senator BARKLEY, but, based upon a friendship and mutual service in the Congress for a period of 23 years, I can say of him as Webster said of Chief Justice Jay:

His character was a rare jewel in the Nation's treasure house of reputation, and the spotless ermine draped upon his shoulders touched nothing less spotless than itself.

Mr. President, it was a gala day for my hometown of Lexington, Va., when Senator BARKLEY arrived there to make the keynote speech at the mock convention at Washington and Lee University. The people of Lexington acclaimed him and the students of Washington and Lee acclaimed him. It was, for him, a familiar setting and a very stimulating one. When he was suddenly stricken by the hand of death everyone in that audience was shocked. They felt they had witnessed an unforgettable tragedy. Indeed, for them it was a tragedy and, likewise, it was a tragedy for the United States Senate, for the State of Kentucky, and for the entire Nation. But to our friend it was not a tragedy, because he endorsed the philosophy of Robert Louis Stevenson who said:

And does not life go down with a better grace to foam in full charge over the precipice than miserably struggling to an end in sandy deltas.

Senator BARKLEY had had a rich career. He aspired to no future honors above those he already held.

Mr. President, I read from the transcript of the speech he delivered at Lexington on the occasion to which I have referred, the very last words he was ever heard to utter:

But I have no longer any personal interest. I have served my country and my people for half a century as a Democrat. I went to the House of Representatives in 1913 and served 14 years. I was a junior Congressman, then I became a senior Congressman, then I went to the Senate and became a junior Senator, and then I became a senior Senator, and then a majority leader of the Senate, and then Vice President of the United States, and now I am back again as a junior Senator.

And I am willing to be a junior. I am glad to sit on the back row. For I would rather be a servant in the House of the Lord than to sit in the seats of the mighty.

That, Mr. President, was the end of a great career, the end of a great statesman, and the end of a beloved friend of us all.

Mr. President, I ask unanimous consent to have printed in the Record at this point in my remarks the text of Senator BARKLEY's extemporaneous remarks as taken down by a reporter on that occasion at the Washington and Lee mock convention.

There being no objection, the address was ordered to be printed in the Record, as follows:

SENATOR ALBEN W. BARKLEY'S LAST SPEECH, WASHINGTON AND LEE UNIVERSITY, APRIL 30, 1956

Governor Stanley, my fellow Americans, and, by the same token, my fellow Democrats, I feel very highly honored, of course, by being chosen as your keynoter and your temporary chairman. I hope my remarks and my appearance and my chairmanship may receive the same approval after I finish that I have had before I start.

It may be that I owe an explanation to Washington and Lee for having attended the law school of the University of Virginia. I have one to give you; I was nurtured in the cradle of Jeffersonian democracy.

I grew up in the same sort of atmosphere in the memory of Andrew Jackson. And I really studied democracy at the feet of Woodrow Wilson. Mrs. Barkley and I are very happy to be here today to be your guests and to be allowed to say a few words on this occasion. As the governor has said, I have been a delegate at large from the State of Kentucky from 1920 until this hour. I have been temporary chairman of 3 of them (conventions), permanent chairman of 1 and took some part in all of them. And I have about concluded that maybe I have gone to enough conventions and I would not go to the one in Chicago this year. But since arriving in Lexington and since arriving in this hall, the old fire horse hears the bell.

And whomever you may nominate here today, I'll be on my way. It is not easy to draw a picture of a great political party that has existed during the entire history of the United States as has the Democratic Party.

Perhaps there has never been an election since 1800, when the author of the Declaration of Independence, the author of Virginia's statute for religious liberty, and the founder of the University of Virginia was elected President—there has never been a year or election since that time when the Democratic Party was not the voice of the people crying from the wilderness in behalf of these same people and the cause which they represent.

Somebody asked me the other day, What is the difference between the Democratic and Republican Parties? And my answer is, The difference between progress and stagnation.

In 1912 Woodrow Wilson stated that the Republican Party had not had a new idea in 40 years. That was 44 years ago, making 84 years in all.

Why do I say that? I say it, because I can with truth ask you here today—or any other convention of either Democrats or Republicans—to name one single great constructive statute that's on the books of the law today that was initiated or inaugurated by the Republican Party.

And as we approach the presidential campaign of 1956, we know you know—the American people know, and the Republican Party knows, it must run on its own record now, and not on the record of someone else.

It was under the administration of Grover Cleveland that the first rural-mail route in America was established. It was under Grover Cleveland that the first act to regulate commerce creating the Interstate Commerce Commission was enacted into law.

I have gone a long way back, but you want the foundation, don't you—for what I said a moment ago.

You don't want me to say anything here today that I can't prove, do you? All right: it was under the administration of Woodrow Wilson that the great Federal Reserve System was established, which enabled us to finance two great wars in the last generation.

It was under the administration of Woodrow Wilson that the Federal Trade Commission was set up, to give a forum where business, large or small, might find a redress for its grievances. I might say that a great Virginian who served in the House and in the Senate and in the Cabinet, of whom I was fond indeed, was one of the constructors of that great economic and financial legislation, the honorable Carter Glass.

It was under the administration of Woodrow Wilson that the greatest tariff law ever enacted in our history was enacted in the Underwood-Simmons tariff law of 1913, which was described as the fairest tariff ever enacted in the history of this Nation.

And it is the only one of the great record of Woodrow Wilson's enactment that the Republicans have ever repealed.

And when they repealed that, they brought on a worldwide, nationwide, panic from which it took a Democratic Party to rescue this Nation in 1933.

It was a Democratic Party that enacted the Clayton antitrust law bringing down to date and up to date the antitrust laws of our country to protect the American people against monopolies and trusts.

It was the Democratic Party that first enacted the highway law, to give aid by the Government of the United States to our States and counties to the building of highways, and that law has been in effect from 1916 until now and now all the Eisenhower administration has been able to do has been to ask us to extend that law and build more highways and we're going to build more than he asks us to build.

It was a Democratic Party that established the Department of Labor, and formed the first Secretary of Labor in the Cabinet of the President of the United States. It was under the leadership of Woodrow Wilson and the Democratic Party that the amendment to the Constitution giving the women of this Nation the right to vote came into effect.

Now, I never thought that women suffrage would bring the millennium. But it couldn't have made it any worse than it was before.

Then came World War I. Following World War I, it was the great President of the United States who tried to bring about peace to the world and to organize mankind in peace instead of war. He gave his life for that cause. And our great domestic program was interfered with by war. And then came the Republicans, which were worse than war. Harding, Coolidge, and Hoover. Now I don't mention those names through any disrespect, for I have respect for anybody elected President of the United States, but I do have to mention them because they did live and were Presidents.

At the end of their 12 years, the American people were in the depths of the greatest economic and social and moral depression in the history of this Nation.

And then what happened? The American people did what they always do when they get in trouble. They called on the Democratic Party to relieve them (from their posts).

Franklin D. Roosevelt became the President of the United States. During his administration more laws were enacted for the benefit of the American people than were ever enacted in any 50 years of our history prior to that time.

I need not here recite them, but I mention merely the Agriculture Adjustment Administration, known as the triple A, which lifted the farmer out of the ditch, and put his feet on solid ground and it is a strange similarity that today that same farmer is in the same ditch, and the Democrats are going to have to lift him out and put him on solid ground again.

It was the same Democratic Party that enacted the law guaranteeing bank deposits of the people of the United States during the 12 years to which I've just referred, bank failures were occurring everywhere all over the Nation.

Due to our foresight, due to our courage, due to the constructive ability of the Democratic Party, we enacted a new banking law and guaranteed the deposits of our people so that they now have faith in their banks and so long as they have faith in their banks there'll be no runs on their banks and no bank failures.

It was the Democratic Party that gave to the Nation and to the world and particularly to the Western Hemisphere the good neighbor policy of Cordell Hull, one of the greatest Secretaries of State in the history of the United States.

Under former Republican administrations we had what we called dollar diplomacy by which was meant our Ambassadors.

(At this point one of the mikes in the hall tipped over with a crash. Senator BARKLEY stopped, smiled and said "that's only a symbol of what is going to happen to the Republicans this fall." This quip brought a roar of laughter and when it subsided the Senator resumed his speech.)

During previous Republican administrations we've had what was called dollar diplomacy which meant that our Ambassadors to our neighbors in South and Central America were sent there largely to exploit those people for the dollars of American investors and American businessmen. Cordell Hull, Tennessee, married a Virginia girl, brought about the good neighbor policy with our neighbors to the south. To show you that the Republicans are trying to keep the same thing but give it a different name, a couple of weeks ago, they unveiled a bust of Cordell Hull in the Pan-American Union Building in Washington. The distinguished gentleman who unveiled him made a speech about him, was unwilling to call it good neighbor policy because it was Democratic. He renamed it the good partner policy.

They've renamed everything, but they've kept it. Now we have the good neighbor policy with our Central and South American neighbors and when we were a second time gone into a World War which we had not caused, against our will, every one of these American Republics joined us in our fights, to preserve democracy, freedom, and the dignity of man. Every great constructive legislative enactment that has found its way to the statutes of American Congress in the last 50 years was put there by the Democratic Party, recommended by Democratic Presidents.

Therefore, I say without any equivocations that the Democratic Party has been the forward-looking, progressive, constructive party in the history of our Nation. It will be as the world goes on now in this great economic struggle to preserve democracy, to hand our Nation down to those who are to come after, the generations to come free and strong, as it was when it came to us, it will be the Democratic Party fighting for the rights of the great masses of our people and not for any particular group of our people.

The great founder of our party was an apostle of equal rights to all, and exclusive privileges to none.

We're for all kind of business so long as it's honest, big or little. We are those who feel that after all in our economic struggle and in the complexity of our lives, Government cannot be indifferent to the welfare of all classes of our people. Therefore, we have a foreign policy, we have a domestic policy, we have a farm policy, we have a labor policy, we have our old-age policy, we have a youth policy. We're not like the Republicans who only have one policy and that's an insurance policy that insures you for what you need and pays you off in everything you got more of than you need.

(One minor sentence was lost at this point due to transmission difficulties.)

But I do know we have an amplitude of worth material. Half a dozen or more, any one of whom would grace the White House and honor the American people with his service.

So, my friends, I'm not going to test your patience by holding you off much longer from the real business of this convention. I want to announce to you that if I had not known it in advance I would have known it when I saw all the floats in the great parade which you put on, but I am myself not a candidate. I have been in years gone by.

I think that I am sufficiently alert to present conditions to know that all fire apparatus are now automotive and not horse drawn.

I have seen the time when I was like old Thomas B. Reed, a man who was Speaker of the House of Representatives back in 1896 when William McKinley was nominated, and he was a candidate. He was known as Czar Reed. He became known as Czar Reed because he was so arbitrary and ruthless in his rulings as a Speaker of the House of Representatives. He was a candidate for the Republican Party for President in 1896. He was getting a very good vote but not enough. Finally a Member of the House came up to the stand and said, "Mr. Speaker, do you think they're going to nominate you out there?" "Well," he said, "my friend, by George, they can go further and do worse and I'm afraid they will."

But I have no longer any personal interest. I have served my country and my people for half a century as a Democrat. I went to the House of Representatives in 1913 and served 14 years. I was a junior Congressman, then I became a senior Congressman, then I went to the Senate and became a junior Senator, and then I became a senior Senator, and then a majority leader of the Senate, and then Vice President of the United States, and now I am back again as a junior Senator.

And I am willing to be a junior. I'm glad to sit on the back row. For I would rather be a servant in the House of the Lord than to sit in the seats of the mighty. (At this point, Senator BARKLEY hesitated, took one step backward, collapsed, and died.)

Mr. NEUBERGER. Mr. President, one of the real privileges which have come to me in the short time I have been a Member of the Senate has been to sit in the back row, over in the corner of the Chamber, near ALBEN BARKLEY. A new Senator or a new locomotive engineer or a new forest ranger is very often dependent on the assistance and counsel of persons having far greater experience and wisdom than himself. I do not believe that any veteran Senator could have been more kind or generous or understanding to a new Senator than ALBEN BARKLEY was to me.

There were many times when I asked him for advice and counsel. He always gave it with unstinted generosity. He was never stingy about his time, although I know there were far more demands upon his time than he could possibly recognize. Yet he often went out of his way to illustrate a point he was making about some particular issue before the Senate with some little episode or epigram or metaphor, which semed to point up his thought. I always marveled at the way he could stand on the Senate floor without a single note or piece of paper in his hand and discuss the most complicated, detailed kind of legislation

In my memory today is one particular occasion when Senator BARKLEY discussed a tariff bill. We all know how technical tariff legislation can be. Yet on that specific occasion Senator BARKLEY went to the very heart of the matter. He discussed import duties, tonnages, and values relating to the particular product which was at issue. I do not recall that he ever consulted a piece of paper or had a note before him.

Senator BARKLEY, I think, illustrated a phrase which the late President Roosevelt once used in referring to Senator

George W. Norris, of Nebraska. President Roosevelt said
that Senator Norris was a man old in years but young in
heart. Certainly that was true, in my opinion, of Senator
ALBEN W. BARKLEY.

I hearken back to an episode which involved not only
Senator BARKLEY but also another man to whom the Senate
is paying tribute today—the late Senator Harley M. Kilgore,
of West Virginia. On the occasion to which I have reference,
Senator Kilgore, who sat in the front row of the Senate, had
offered Senator BARKLEY his chair. The story goes that
Senator Kilgore felt it was not quite appropriate that a man
who had been for so long a Member of both Houses of Congress, who had been the majority leader, and who had been
the Vice President of the United States—that a man having
such an outstanding record as that should occupy a seat in
the back row. Therefore, Senator Kilgore had offered to
exchange his seat in the front row for Senator BARKLEY's seat
in the back row.

Senator BARKLEY came back and told Senator Patrick Mc-
Namara and me about Senator Kilgore's very kind offer.
Then Senator BARKLEY said, "I told Harley that I like it back
there so well with the freshman Senators, Pat and Dick, that
I think I will just stay back there with them."

No matter how long or how brief may be my tenure in the
Senate, I think that is one of the best compliments I shall
ever receive. I feel certain that Senator McNamara also will
agree that it will rank at the top of any accolades he may
collect.

Mr. President, I think Senator BARKLEY died as he would
have wished to die. He was standing in a great forum at
a great, traditional college in the South. He was addressing
young persons whose futures were still before them. He
was talking about the glories of our country and the glories
of the Democratic Party. In that instant death overtook
him. The exact episode of his passing and the atmosphere
of his passing were recalled to Mrs. Neuberger and me a few

days later, when we attended the funeral of Senator BARK-LEY at Foundry Methodist Church, where a most eloquent and moving eulogy in tribute to Senator BARKLEY was delivered by our beloved friend, the Chaplain of the Senate, the Reverend Dr. Frederick Brown Harris.

Sitting in the front row directly in front of Mrs. Neuberger and me was Senator Theodore Francis Green, who only a few days ago became the oldest Member of the United States Senate in the entire history of our country. As we walked out of the church I remarked to Senator Green, "This must be a sad day for you, Senator Green, because you and Senator BARKLEY were friends for so long a time and served so long together in the Senate."

Senator Green looked at us, smiled, and said, "No; this is not a sad day; it is a glorious day." He added, "Is it not fine that Senator BARKLEY died on the stump, on the rostrum, while he was still in the full possession of all his powers of intellect and physique, and that he did not waste away agonizingly in some hospital bed?"

As Mrs. Neuberger and I walked away from the church after leaving Senator Green, we commented on how descriptive was that remark, not only of ALBEN W. BARKLEY, but also of Senator Green, our colleague.

Mr. President, it has been a great privilege for me, a new Member of the Senate, to have served, if only for a brief time, with a person so distinguished, so kind, so wise as ALBEN BARKLEY. Fortunate, indeed, is that country which has representatives who served without selfishness and without fear.

Mr. GEORGE. Mr. President, I rise to pay an unstudied tribute to my friend, ALBEN BARKLEY. He was in Georgia, in college, during my college years, although we were not at the same school nor in the same town.

When I came to Washington, he was a Member of the House, and had been for a number of years. About 5 years after I entered the Senate, the then Representative BARKLEY was elected to the Senate. I served with him when he was the majority leader and the minority leader of his party. I had a close association with him as a member of the Committee on Finance. I was a member of the Committee on Finance when ALBEN BARKLEY came to the Senate, but I soon learned to know him much better as a fellow committeeman. Our relationships were always pleasant and cordial.

A little later, he became a member of the Committee on Foreign Relations, and as a member of that committee he was always quite willing to assume his full responsibilities. He did not duck issues; he always voted his convictions.

Senator BARKLEY was not deceived by temporary changes in the currents, the tides, or the winds, because he seemed to have an appreciation of something far more fundamental and far more enduring. As a member of the Committee on Finance and also of the Committee on Foreign Relations, he was always diligent in the discharge of his immediate duties, and was always highly honorable in his appreciation of the great issues which came before those two committees.

It is significant, because it serves to teach us how fleeting a thing is life itself, to realize that today we are paying tribute to two honorable men who served in this body but a little while ago—Harley Kilgore, of West Virginia, a kindly disposed man, cordial in his relationships with his fellows here; and ALBEN BARKLEY, who had a due, fine, and high appreciation of life.

I think I may be pardoned for saying that what always impressed me most about ALBEN BARKLEY—and my association with him was close, so close that almost daily we had lunch together during the present session of the Congress— was his lack of malice. ALBEN BARKLEY was incapable of malice. He bore no malice toward any man. He bore no malice toward any political party, although he was in sharp disagreement with the policies of parties other than his own. But he was wholly incapable of possessing the uncomfortable, unhappy attribute which we describe as malice. He did not agree, and made no pretense of agreeing, to things in which he did not believe. He was outspoken, he was strong in the assertion of his own political faith, but he lacked malice; and nothing petty, nothing trifling, nothing ignoble ever darkened his mind or his heart.

ALBEN BARKLEY was a man who deserved greatly of his day and his generation. He served his State well. He served his country well. He was almost universally beloved through the Nation, because everyone knew intuitively that littleness of soul and malice of heart were utterly foreign to his nature.

And so, Mr. President, I simply pay my unsteadied tribute to the live, vibrant human soul who so lately was here among us. I do not forget the last moment when I parted with ALBEN BARKLEY at the home of Senator Harry Byrd, in Virginia, from which home he went to the last engagement he had. And I do not forget that he told me he would be out of Washington on Monday, but that he thought he would get back on Tuesday. But he did not come back. A little more than a month before his going, he had promised to accompany me to Georgia. He promised to go with me to the beautiful queen city of northeast Georgia and to make a speech at what has been called the poultry festival of the southeast, in that community and in that area of the State. We discussed it on more than 1 day. I anxiously awaited the time when he would make that trip, because he would be talking to people very much like his people in Kentucky. He would be talking to the hill people and the mountain people of northeast Georgia. He would be talking to friends, because some of them had gone to college with Senator BARKLEY in Georgia, and vast scores had met him in after life.

ALBEN BARKLEY presented, on the whole, a man whose likeness we do not see now in our Chamber, nor will we be likely to see it for many, many days to come. He loved his State, as I have said. He loved his country. He loved his party, but in no spirit of narrowness. He loved his party because he thought his party represented the best interest of his country and the best interest of humanity.

Of course, men do not always agree in this body, but on the two committees to which I have referred, where he was serving even at the time of his death—although on his return to the Senate he had been passed over for men who had the claim of seniority to those committee places—I do not recall any occasion, however sharp the issue, when there was any disagreement or difference of viewpoint that meant any estrangement or even straining of cordial personal relations between us.

I early learned that ALBEN BARKLEY viewed all mankind with the sort of deep and abiding and universal love that men feel for their fellow men when their own hearts are right. I listened to his stories by the hour. I listened to his wisdom with great profit. I know he made a great contribution to his day and to his generation.

In point of years, ALBEN BARKLEY was but a few months older than the senior Senator from Georgia. In point of wisdom and experience, he was very much my senior. In point of deep affection and feeling, I shall always be happy until the end that we shared a friendship which was unselfish and which was mutually helpful. However, I was the chief beneficiary of that happy friendship, which began many, many long years ago, and which lasted down to the end. I revere ALBEN BARKLEY's memory, I esteem his friendship as one of the most precious possessions in my life and in my experience. I esteem his kindly and his gentle feeling. I esteem the indulgence that a great man can always show to any of his fellow men, however weak. I think of him in times when we were in disagreement and in times when we were in agreement; but I always think of him as a genuine American who loved his country well.

Mr. President, let me quote the words of a distinguished Georgian, who once served with great honor in this body, before I came to it:

He who saves his country saves all things, lives nobly, and all things saved bless him.

He who lets his country die, lets all things die, dies himself ignobly, and all things dying curse him.

ALBEN BARKLEY lived well—lived well with his country, with his family, with peace, and with his God—because he always sought to save his country. Regardless of whatever the cost might have been to him at the moment, he sought to save his country and to preserve it.

He has left a legacy which those who bear his name may always regard with the pride of generations who have followed great men who served and who loved their country.

Mr. ERVIN. Mr. President, I should like to associate myself with the very beautiful remarks made by the beloved and distinguished senior Senator from Georgia [Mr. George] in reference to our departed colleagues, whom we remember today.

I should like to add only a word or two. Senator ALBEN W. BARKLEY was undoubtedly one of the most remarkable men in the history of our Nation. He alined himself in a positive fashion on the issues which confronted the Nation during his day. I think we can say of him, as the poet said of his friend:

Green be the grass above thee, friend of our better days;
None knew thee but to love thee, nor named thee but to praise.

That certainly applies to Senator BARKLEY.

As the distinguished senior Senator from Georgia has pointed out, everyone who knew Senator BARKLEY loved him. Although Senator BARKLEY lived in the center of great controversies, no one ever spoke of him except in terms of the highest praise.

Mr. MONRONEY. Mr. President, it is an honor to be allowed to associate one's self with the remarks made here today in memory of the great public service rendered by the beloved ALBEN W. BARKLEY, to whom I shall always refer as Vice President ALBEN BARKLEY, and by the distinguished Senator Harley Kilgore, of West Virginia. As a younger

Member of the United States Senate, it was a privilege to know these men and to know that in the midst of the heavy workload that was upon them—in Senator Barkley's case, as Vice President of the United States; and in the case of Senator Kilgore, as chairman of the powerful and overworked Judiciary Committee—they always had time to extend a helping hand to a young man who was trying to adjust himself to the troubles and perplexities of service in this great legislative body.

Mr. President, often when I am showing young people from Oklahoma about the Capitol—for instance, today I had the privilege of escorting in the Capitol Building two representatives from the Girls Nation—I take occasion to take them into the old Senate Chamber, in the old part of the Capitol Building, and show them the desks of Calhoun, Webster, and the other greats of past years, who have made their imprint upon the security and the very existence of our Nation. I often wonder whether any of those "giants" who once walked the floor of the United States Senate, would have been able to write a record any greater, if as great, as that written by Alben W. Barkley during his service in the legislative halls of the Nation from 1912 until this year of 1956.

Alben W. Barkley was a man with great good humor, with great competence, with deep and abiding respect for the intelligence of all the people of the United States, and for our system of representative democracy. I wonder whether any of the "giants" of the past could have exceeded the contributions and accomplishments of Alben W. Barkley, in solving the problems of their day; whether they could have contributed to the welfare of the Nation in greater degree than did Alben W. Barkley, during his magnificent service in World War I, as a Member of the House of Representatives, and subsequently as a Member of the United States Senate; and, during the postwar period, when efforts were made, under the Great Woodrow Wilson, to establish a world organization—the League of Nations—and then in helping, as Senator BARKLEY did so greatly, to bring the Nation from its lassitude during peace to a posture of greater defense efforts before the outbreak of World War II, and the subsequent bombing of Pearl Harbor; and then, during the war, in helping to bring about the strengthening of our Nation and its defense; and, following that, in his strong leadership, as majority leader, in connection with the passage of measures which made possible our adherence to the United Nations and our contributions in that field; and subsequently, during the postwar period, in his outstanding service as Vice President of the United States.

I doubt that any man outside of the Presidency or the position of Secretary of State could have done more than did Senator ALBEN BARKLEY to bring about the influence that America enjoyed during the postwar period. In that connection, let me refer to the Marshall plan, the Greek-Turkish aid prorgam, and all the other things which Senator BARKLEY, as majority leader of the United States Senate, helped to bring to reality.

Senator BARKLEY's great good humor made him appreciated, honored, and respected by all America. All Americans followed him day by day because he had the gracious gift of good humor, because he always had a "homey" story to illustrate the issues facing the Nation.

I shall never forget the untiring work he performed. I had the good fortune of serving with him on several conference committees, while I was a member of the House of Representatives and while he was majority leader of the Senate. I also served with him on 1 or 2 other committees, including the Senate Committee on Banking and Currency. I well remember that during the long conferences over inflation-control legislation, Senator BARKLEY would meet with us from 10 o'clock in the morning until perhaps 4 o'clock in the afternoon, and then often would express his apologies for having to fulfill an important speaking engagement—perhaps in Chicago or in Buffalo—that evening. He would fly all night, to return to his post of duty early next morning in the committees and also in the Senate Chamber, where he was always prepared to exercise his splendid abilities as majority leader. I constantly marveled at his endurance, his breadth of vision, his capability, his accumulation and use of information. I constantly admired the great ability he had, which permitted him to make such outstanding contributions to the Congress and to the Nation during those years of his notable leadership in this body.

I trust that the tradition of ALBEN BARKLEY will continue to be one of the guiding lights of the United States. He was a man who could disagree without being disagreeable; a man who could always find a point in any situation, no matter how tense, at which to break out the good humor which is native to the American spirit of fair play and common-sense.

I am grateful for the opportunity of expressing my appreciation of the distinguished service of ALBEN W. BARKLEY.

Mr. CURTIS. Mr. President, I could not hope to make any considerable contribution to the tributes which have been paid to two departed Senators by those who served with them for so long. Nevertheless, I wish to join in expressing my appreciation for the service which they rendered. Throughout the greater portion of my lifetime the late ALBEN W. BARKLEY has been a prominent figure in American public life. He has brought distinction and honor to this body, and we shall always cherish his memory.

Mr. WELKER. Mr. President, no word I might say could match the beautiful tributes which have been paid to the distinguished late Vice President and our colleague, ALBEN W. BARKLEY. So I wish to join my colleagues, and associate myself with their remarks.

Aside from the sacred things in my life, ALBEN W. BARKLEY bestowed upon me the greatest honor it has been my privilege to receive. He administered to me the oath of office as a United States Senator. My heart, like those of my colleagues assembled here today, is full of memories of ALBEN W. BARKLEY. There is nothing human hands or human minds can do to alleviate the suffering caused by the departure of that great statesman.

I shall never forget his manifold kindnesses to me as a new Senator, even though I was of the opposite political faith. At times I served as acting minority leader, when he was Vice President or President pro tempore. He was very kind about helping those of us who knew little about parliamentary procedures. Many times he would step down from the Vice President's chair and come to my desk to talk with me and help me in connection with problems about which I knew very little.

I can say with the utmost confidence that the memory of the great ALBEN W. BARKLEY will be cherished by Republicans as well as Democrats. He was dedicated to a cause which he thought was right. No greater tribute could be paid to any man. He was truly a statesman, even though at times I disagreed with him. If we always agreed upon every question, this would not be much of a legislative body.

ALBEN W. BARKLEY was a statesman. As has been previously stated, he served his country through some of the most trying times of the Republic—through World War I, World War II, the Korean war, and many other difficult periods. He leaves to us as Senators a heritage which I hope we can appreciate. He leaves to us an example which we can try to follow. In my opinion, no Member of this body could do better than to try to emulate the example of the great ALBEN W. BARKLEY in his service to his country and to his State.

I shall never be convinced that ALBEN W. BARKLEY is dead. He is only away.

Mr. MORSE. Mr. President, I know that every Senator who has paid tribute to HARLEY KILGORE and ALBEN BARKLEY today is filled with a deep sense of humility, and also with a deep sense of debt and gratitude for the opportunity which has been ours of association with these two great statesmen.

I use the term "statesmen" advisedly, although I recognize that in our time too frequently it is used loosely.

These men, judged by their records, by their lives, and by their services—which, after all, constitute their historic monuments—in my judgment met the three criteria of statesmanship. There are three essential elements which must exist before one can possibly qualify as a statesman.

The first is integrity, character which meets the fiery test of temptation.

The second is courage. These men lived it and exemplified it.

The third is brains; and there is no substitute for brains in public service.

These two statesmen evidenced time and again the indispensable attribute of high intelligence.

I recognize, Mr. President, that political labels can become meaningless as the result of careless use. However, I believe here we have two statesmen to whom the term "liberal" can be properly applied if the term be used in the definitive sense in which I use it. They were men who by their legislative endeavors sought to promote the welfare of the people of our country. That is the legislative objective of liberals. Liberals recognize the superiority of human values over materialism. They recognize the importance of promoting the welfare of the people rather than of enhancing the profits of economic groups, motivated by selfishness.

One needs only to turn to the legislative record of HARLEY KILGORE and ALBEN BARKLEY to see how inescapable the conclusion I now submit really is. These men worked for the people. They recognized that that is the primary obligation of a Senator.

Their footprints are so deeply imprinted on the floor of the Senate that they will never be eroded, no matter how long the passage of time.

I remember the last day that the great BARKLEY served in this Chamber. During that afternoon he came over and sat alongside of me, and his wit and good humor were at their best. He said, "Wayne, what are you doing here? I never learned how to win elections in Kentucky by staying in Washington."

It happened that at the time I had a contest in the primary in the State of Oregon. We had a good laugh about it. I pointed out to him that there chanced to be pending in the Senate some legislation to be considered in the near future, which was of vital concern to my State, and I was remaining in the Senate to participate in the discussion of it. The Record will show that I did. That explanation Senator BARKLEY was willing to accept for my presence in the Senate at the time, even though he felt I ought to be taking part in the campaign in my State.

I wonder how many people fully appreciate the fact that ALBEN BARKLEY was a keen student of the Scriptures. On various occasions I heard him discuss with great scholarship Biblical history. It was in one of those discussions that I learned that one of his favorite passages in the Book of Life was the psalm which I shall read as my closing tribute to this great statesman and this good Christian. ALBEN BARKLEY was particularly fond of the Twenty-third Psalm. The Twenty-third Psalm is a particularly fitting tribute to the life of this great American. I read it in memory of ALBEN BARKLEY:

The Lord is my shepherd; I shall not want.
He maketh me to lie down in green pastures: He leadeth me beside the still waters.
He restoreth my soul: He leadeth me in the paths of righteousness for His name's sake.
Yea, though I walk through the valley of the shadow of death, I will fear no evil: for Thou art with me; Thy rod and Thy staff they comfort me.
Thou preparest table before me in the presence of mine enemies: Thou anointest my head with oil; my cup runneth over.

Surely goodness and mercy shall follow me all the days of my life: and I will dwell in the house of the Lord for ever.

Mr. O'MAHONEY. Mr. President, recognizing, as I do, my inability to pay adequate tribute to either of the great statesmen whom we memorialize today, I nevertheless cannot allow the hour to pass without adding a word to what has been said.

I remember well when Senator BARKLEY was elected majority leader of the Senate. I know that history will record the fact that he served as majority leader of the Senate longer than any other man. That service came during one of the gravest and most critical periods of our Nation's history. I served with him during that entire period, and from my place upon the floor I observed his work. I marveled at his ability to acquaint himself with all essential knowledge respecting every measure which came under his leadership.

Mr. President, he was a man who had a masterly grasp of the facts and a clear understanding of law and of logic. His equal, I am sure, certainly, his superior, never walked the floor of the Senate of the United States. This I say because I saw Senator BARKLEY at work. I saw him at work as Vice President. He will be recorded among the great men of our Nation's history. I am proud to be able to say that he was my friend. I deeply regretted his passing. The Senate and the Nation have lost a magnificent public servant.

Mr. WATKINS. Mr. President, no man who has sat in this Hall of Congress in recent years can think back on the late distinguished Senator ALBEN WILLIAM BARKLEY without a smile and a tear. In his high and constant good humor, in his joy in the story well told, the junior Senator from Kentucky was a constant delight. Yet Senator BARKLEY was not just a teller of tales, but a man of understanding and discernment whose practical wisdom and well-considered judgment were of ever-sought value to the Senate and the people.

In a sense, in Senator BARKLEY a chapter of American life was represented. He came into the practice of law in the first months of the new century, and rose successively through local offices to the Congress, where more than 20 sessions ago his voice was first heard. Through the twenties, thirties, forties—those memorable years—he sat in these Halls of Congress, an eager participant in the debate of those days. In him, then, the first half of the 20th century has a congressional counterpart.

There is no doubting Paducah's love for her native son, and the affection in which he was held by his State of Kentucky. America, too, shares this affection, for no matter how hard the fray, how embattled the issues, Senator BARKLEY remained a kindly force, working for the right as he saw it.

Now that he has gone home—to his last rest—we may be sad. But not for long would ALBEN BARKLEY have seen us this way. His joyful spirit could not long contain the spirit of sadness.

Proceedings
in the
House of Representatives

Proceedings in the House

The SPEAKER. The Chair recognizes the gentleman from Kentucky [Mr. Spence].

Mr. SPENCE. Mr. Speaker, it is my very sad duty to announce the death on yesterday of Kentucky's most distinguished citizen, Senator ALBEN W. BARKLEY. Senator BARKLEY served his State and his Nation with great ability and great distinction for 43 years. He was a superb statesman and an unselfish patriot. Death came while he was addressing a college audience which was holding a mock Democratic convention.

Senator BARKLEY, like Abraham Lincoln, was born in a log cabin in Kentucky. And, like Abraham Lincoln, he had to overcome these disadvantages. Because of his poverty he was compelled to earn his bread while he received his education. His genial personality, his kindly and companionable nature endeared him to all the people of Kentucky. He had a delightful wit that loved to play, not wound. Today Kentucky has a heavy heart because of his death. He had lived more than 3 score years and 10, but it is sad that men of his character and his ability should pass away while they are in possession of their fine faculties and judgment.

He served in this House for 14 years, and then he went to the Senate where he was serving his fifth term. In the Senate he became the majority leader where he displayed splendid ability and highest quality of leadership. He then became Vice President of the United States, which gave the people of the Nation an opportunity to know him. I am sure they had somewhat the same affection for him as the people of his native State. We have indeed sustained a great loss. He died as I know he would like to have gone—not from a bed of pain and suffering and sickness, but with his spirits high and the applause and laughter of his audience ringing in his ears. He fell as the mighty unbending oak falls before the whirlwind in the forest.

His last words were a prayer. He said, "I would rather be a servant in the house of the Lord than to sit in the seats of the mighty." He was a faithful servant to the people he represented through his long career. He will be a faithful servant in the house of the Lord, and I know that the light of the countenance of his Master will shine upon him and give him peace.

To his devoted wife and his family, I extend my deepest sympathy.

Mr. CHELF. Mr. Speaker, will the gentleman yield?

Mr. SPENCE. I yield to the gentleman from Kentucky.

Mr. CHELF. Mr. Speaker, this is a sad day for Paducah, a sorrowful day for McCracken County, an unhappy day for all of Kentucky, and a horrible blow for the Nation and the world. We down in Kentucky have lost not only a great man, an outstanding citizen, a foremost American, an extraordinary legislator, but one of the finest, one of the sweetest, one of the most lovable persons who ever walked under the broad, blue canopy of God's own heaven.

Senator BARKLEY's life was indeed a story of Horatio Alger. Born of humble parents in a log cabin down in western Kentucky, his father in the great panic of 1890 lost his farm and became a tenant farmer. Young BARKLEY was inspired by reading the lives of Lincoln, Washington, and other great Americans. He wanted to make something of his life, and his friends encouraged him and they advised his father to send him away to school. Since his father was not able to do so ALBEN worked his way through by doing the job of janitor on the school buildings. One of the old buildings of the college, that is today being used as a hotel, now has a sign out that reads: "BARKLEY swept here." At the age of only 20 years he won his first oratorical contest.

Shortly thereafter his good friends and neighbors, the people of McCracken County, honored him by electing him their county attorney, then their county judge. Later he ran for a seat in this great body and was sent here for 14 years—7 different terms. Then he decided he would try for the governorship of Kentucky, and that, Mr. Speaker, is the only race in which he ever suffered a bitter disappointment. He was nosed out by a few votes. But he came back the very next year with his determination, his grit, with his ability, and by that time he was better known statewide, and he won the Democratic nomination for United States Senator and was elected in that November by one of the greatest majorities any Kentuckian has ever rolled up running for office.

He served in the Senate for 22 long fruitful years, during 11 of which, Mr. Speaker, he bore upon his back and upon his conscience the majority leadership. This was during the war years, when it was necessary to get the money for planes, tanks, and the guns to equip our boys. He was fighting for our freedom and Christianity and all that it means, just as surely as our boys were fighting in the war for it. His assignment as majority leader was enough to kill any 10 men, but, Mr. Speaker, ALBEN BARKLEY put his shoulder to the task and his heart to the challenge, and he came through, as you know, with flying colors, and history has so recorded it.

Mr. Speaker, there is very little I can add. The people of Kentucky loved him, the people of the Nation respected and admired him because they elected him Vice President of the United States, and he served ably and well in that high office.

Mr. Speaker, somehow I feel today that but for his character, his honesty, he could have been President of the United States. Why? Because when the challenge came, when courage was needed, he saw fit to take issue with the then President. He did so and he was unafraid. He made a speech on the floor of the Senate in which he violently disagreed with the then President over a tax veto. In my humble opinion, from the bottom of my heart, I believe that this cost him the Vice Presidential nod and therefor later the very Presidency itself. I later said to him when I was talking to him about it: "Senator, you could have been President if you had not made that speech, and if after making it you had not resigned as majority leader of the United States Senate." He said: "Frank, I know in my heart that I was right, and I would rather be right than to be President of the United States of America."

That was the creed and that was the belief that was the life of ALBEN W. BARKLEY. And as my great and distinguished friend the gentleman from Kentucky [Mr. Spence] has just said, the folks wanted him to continue in office. He wanted to retire back home in Kentucky with his friends and his family. Friends of Mr. Spence and myself, friends of every Member of the Kentucky delegation were asking us to ask him to run again. They wanted to see him back on the Hill, they felt that they needed at this time, of all times in our history, a man of courage, honor, one of ability; one with know-how—he did run. He was nominated by an overwhelming majority and he defeated a fine Kentucky Republican to win back again his old Senate seat.

Senator BARKLEY, the one and only great "Veep" died as I know he wanted to, with his boots on. He had almost finished his speech. And there is another thing that stands out indelibly on his magnificent record of achievement—with diamond words emblazoned in a golden book on silver pages, his great love for his fellow man, his love for young people. He was appearing at a mock convention to help these young college students to learn more about the government of our great country—how our great two-party system operates and how it has succeeded.

Mr. Speaker, I could go on, but suffice it to say that we have lost a great American. I would like to say to you that when he came down to campaign in my great Fourth District in 1954, I went with him on every stump. Yes, we campaigned together. We had a lot of fun. He was a wonderful companion and my dear friend, and I like to call him not only my friend, but also my buddy. To show how considerate he was of others—he often told me that I should not work so hard making so many speeches for him. He would say: "Frank, you have no opposition at all—you are just out of the hospital and major surgery—take it easy, my boy." It was an inspiration to just be with him. I would hold my side and my scars when he was not looking—and proceed to pour it on as best I could for him. He carried my district by over 10,000 votes. We both were so pleased over it.

One of the stories he told I think is apropos to tell here because everyone knows how he would feel if he were here now. He would want us not to feel bad today, believe me, and I say that from the bottom of my heart. This is one of the stories he told that everyone loved so well, and it was one of his favorites.

Back many years ago when he was a boy on the farm, his father needed a timepiece, a clock. It was a long way to the county seat, Paducah. In those days you had to use a horse and buggy to get there. So his father sent him over to the adjoining farm to borrow a clock from one of his neighbors who had several clocks. He brought it back home. But they were always in a state of confusion over the clock. They could not tell the time by that clock. Finally Senator BARKLEY took the clock back to the neighbor and told him about it. His neighbor said, "ALBEN, I am sorry about that clock. You know, I forgot to tell you that when both hands point to high noon and the clock strikes 3, that means it is 6 o'clock."

Yes, that was one of his favorite stories. I could go on and tell you many great things about this great individual. He has so conducted himself amongst his fellow men, he has let his light so shine, that his fellow men might plainly see his good works and glorify our Father who is in heaven.

He has created with his own hands, his high station in life. He has built a monument higher, brighter, whiter and more beautiful, if you please, than the Washington Monument, in my opinion.

Mr. Speaker, I extend to his good wife, Mrs. Barkley, to his children and his grandchildren my deepest sympathy and may God rest him and keep him in peace. The Master would say: "Well done, thou good and faithful servant; enter into the kingdom. I have a special place for you."

Mr. PERKINS. Mr. Speaker, will the gentleman yield?

Mr. SPENCE. I yield to the gentleman from Kentucky [Mr. Perkins].

Mr. PERKINS. Mr. Speaker, the news of ALBEN BARKLEY'S death last night was a shock to the whole world. Senator BARKLEY was a dear friend to all peaceloving nations.

I, like all Kentuckians, received this news with the deepest of sorrow. I readily realized not only the great loss the State of Kentucky had sustained but also the Nation. The same feeling was being expressed by every Kentuckian that I met last night in Ashland after we received this sad and shocking news. All Kentuckians loved ALBEN BARKLEY. They loved him because he was a man of principle and an individual the ordinary layman could look to for inspiration.

It will serve no useful purpose for me to mention the outstanding and unexcelled contributions that ALBEN BARKLEY has made in the field of government, except I want to say that, in my judgment, this country has never produced a greater public servant and statesman than Senator BARKLEY, or a man that has contributed more to the general welfare of all the people in this Nation.

Kentucky, as well as the Nation, has suffered an irreparable loss. Senator BARKLEY's last words, "I am willing to be a junior. I am glad to sit on the back row, for I had rather be a servant in the house of the Lord than to sit in the seats of the mighty," preceding his untimely and unexpected death, discloses not only his Christian qualities but that he was a man of unimpeachable integrity.

I have been a close personal friend of ALBEN BARKLEY's since 1932, and I loved him just like hundreds of thousands of other Kentuckians. I recall distinctly when he first displayed his oratorical ability in my hometown in the year of 1923 when he was a candidate for the Democratic nomination for governor. He was a companionable person, which I feel is a great asset to one in public service; a public servant that you could go to for advice and always receive wise counsel.

Mr. Speaker, the untimely passing of Senator BARKLEY has not only aggrieved and left me with an overwhelming sense of personal loss but has brought the same feeling to all the people in Kentucky, which ALBEN BARKLEY loved with all his his heart.

We all take pride in paying tribute to our great public servants. America and Kentucky never have had a more sincere or devoted public servant. To his wife and all the members of his family I extend not only my deepest sympathy but the deepest sympathy of all the people that I am privileged to represent who knew and loved Senator ALBEN BARKLEY better than any other man in public life in this day and age.

Mr. SPENCE. Mr. Speaker, I yield to the gentleman from Kentucky [Mr. Natcher].

Mr. NATCHER. Mr. Speaker, I rise to pay humble tribute to the memory of my friend and fellow Kentuckian, ALBEN W. BARKLEY. His death removes from this earth one of Kentucky's great statesmen, and a man recognized throughout the world as a leader of men and a man of public spirit. He was a great orator, and a perfect gentleman. A kind considerate man whose exemplary life influenced his own generation and succeeding generations.

Senator BARKLEY served for over 40 years in the Congress of the United before being elected Vice President on November 2, 1948, for the term beginning January 20, 1949. A man of fine judgment with the courage to carry out his convictions, a true public servant. As a great Kentuckian and public servant he again answered the call of his people after his term for Vice President expired when he was elected to the United States Senate for the term beginning January 3, 1955. Throughout his long career as a legislator he was a friend of the farmer, the working people, small business, industry, our professions, and the veterans. In private life he gained success as a lawyer and a farmer. In every position he held, either private or public, he achieved distinction. His service in all of his assignments was marked by a high sense of conscience and duty. He loved people, and they, in turn, loved him. The qualities which endeared ALBEN W. BARKLEY to those who knew him were his devotion to his family and friends, his rugged integrity, and his unfailing sense of humor and good commonsense. His contributions to better government were many and will long be remembered.

The Commonwealth of Kentucky and the United States have lost a great statesman and leader. I have lost a true friend. A friend who lived his life fully and served his country well. To his wife, his children, and grandchildren, Senator ALBEN W. BARKLEY left a proud heritage. I extend to them my deepest sympathy in their bereavement.

Mr. GREGORY. Mr. Speaker, you know that the hearts of all Kentuckians are heavy and our heads are bowed in grief over the passing of our most illustrious native son. I particularly am grieved over the loss of this great and good friend. He was a resident of the great First District of Kentucky, which I have the honor to represent and which he made a great district as an illustrious Member of the House, as a distinguished Senator from Kentucky, and later as the Vice President. His last words were typical of him and typified his life both as a citizen, as a neighbor, and as a public official. I am sure that I have known him longer than any Member of either body as I knew him when I was a small boy and witnessed his climb in public affairs from county office to the pinnacle in national affairs in his party and in his Nation.

ALBEN BARKLEY was born in the small community of Lowes, in Graves County, Ky. He never forgot his beginning in humble surroundings and his loyalty to that community and his devotion never wavered.

I felt that it would be appropriate that the high school at Lowes, Ky., should have the flag which was flown at half mast over the House from which he started his rise to fame. I have sent this flag to the Lowes, Ky., High School with the accompanying letter:

To the Students of Lowes High School, Lowes, Ky.:

The hearts of all of us in Kentucky and, in fact, throughout the Nation are heavy and our heads are bowed in sorrow over the sudden passing of the late Senator ALBEN W. BARKLEY whose life has for so many years been dedicated to unselfish public service to his fellowman.

I know that in his birthplace of Lowes his loss is probably felt more keenly, if possible, than elsewhere. His loyalty and devotion to the Lowes community never wavered. Your forebears knew him as a schoolboy and knew of his ambition, character, and determination to be of service to his fellowman. He realized this ambition and achieved the second highest honor in the world in becoming the most popular Vice President in the history of the United States.

Coming from a modest beginning and having achieved these many great honors by the application of industry and honesty—fortified by character and unselfishness, his life was and will always be a beacon light of inspiration to young men and women possessing these traits.

The Congress of the United States paid just tribute to him. All flags were flown at half mast when his passing was announced. Since he started his rise to fame as a Member of the House of Representatives, I feel that the flag flown over the House of Representatives at half mast should be presented to you to hang in your school as a constant reminder to you and the students of the generations yet to come that great good can be achieved by you if you emulate his great life. I am sure that this will be an inspiration to you.

I have secured this flag and am sending it to you today together with a certificate of the Clerk of the House that this is the authentic flag flown over the House at half mast as a token of grief and deep respect which not only the Congress felt but which was shared by peoples of the entire world.

So long, Mr. Speaker, as character and devotion are honored among men, so long as courage of conviction may be cherished among men, so long as unselfish service to humanity is appreciated—just so long will the memory of ALBEN W. BARKLEY occupy a hallowed place in the minds and hearts of all Americans.

Mr. SPENCE. Mr. Speaker, I yield to the gentleman from Kentucky [Mr. Siler].

Mr. SILER. Mr. Speaker, it was the poet, Alfred Tennyson, who gave us those lines Crossing the Bar:

> Sunset and evening star,
>   And one clear call for me!
> And may there be no moaning of the bar,
>   When I put out to sea.
> But such a tide as moving seems asleep,
>   Too full for sound and foam,
> When that which drew from out the boundless deep
>   Turns again home.
> Twilight and evening bell,
>   And after that the dark!
> And may there be no sadness of farewall,
>   When I embark;
> For though from out our bourne of Time and Place
>   The flood may bear me far,
> I hope to see my Pilot face to face
>   When I have crossed the bar.

Mr. Speaker, my fellow Kentuckian was a good man and I am confident that as he goes out to meet his Pilot face to face, he will be able to give a good accounting of his stewardship and of a life well spent and work well done.

Mr. SPENCE. Mr. Speaker, at this time I yield to the distinguished gentleman from Indiana [Mr. Halleck].

Mr. HALLECK. Mr. Speaker, all of us here today, on both sides of the aisle, are touched with sadness at the death of one who had been a beloved colleague for so many years, first in this Chamber and then in the other body.

ALBEN BARKLEY was a stalwart and honorable warrior of the political arena whose devotion to his country was unquestioned by all who knew him.

ALBEN BARKLEY took the responsibilities of his office seriously, which was fitting and proper.

But he never let the burdens of public service overwhelm his wonderful sense of humor.

He was a charming companion, whose colorful personality and gift for story telling will long be remembered by all who were fortunate enough to enjoy his acquaintance.

Those of us who have fought this battle longest will best appreciate ALBEN BARKLEY's loyalty to the cause in which he believed.

We will best appreciate and understand his rugged partisanship, which gave way only when, in his opinion, such deviation was dictated by the national welfare.

We on the Republican side honored and respected ALBEN BARKLEY as a fair and worthy opponent.

We admired his many talents, and we felt a great affection for him as a generous, kindly, and thoughtful friend.

We shall miss ALBEN BARKLEY. Yet the shock of his sudden passing is eased somewhat in the knowledge that his was a long and distinguished career—which is a privilege not all of us can hope to enjoy—and that the end, when it came, was apparently without great suffering or heavy pain.

Mr. SPENCE. Mr. Speaker, Senator BARKLEY and the Speaker of this House served long together. I know Senator BARKLEY had a very great devotion to and warm friendship for our Speaker. I know that was reciprocated by Speaker Rayburn.

At this time I yield to our distinguished Speaker.

Mr. RAYBURN. Mr. Speaker, in 1913 ALBEN BARKLEY and I stood in this well and took the oath of office. We were assigned to the same committee, the Committee on Interstate and Foreign Commerce, where he served with me for 14 years. He went to the Senate, and in 1937 when I was elected majority leader of the House of Representatives he was elected majority leader of the Senate. I became presiding officer in the House and he became the presiding officer in the Senate. That is the parallel that he and I discussed many times and always with great pleasure, because he knew of my deep devotion to him and I knew of his deep devotion to me.

ALBEN BARKLEY had the good elements mixed in him I think, as many as any man it has been my privilege to know. God gave him a sturdy stature physically and mentality that was big, and he did things with his physical and his mental capacity. I think that ALBEN BARKLEY was probably the greatest orator we have produced in a quarter of a century. He had a way about him of getting his story over in sincerity and with sound judgment.

He was a statesman of the first order. He will rank and deserves to rank with the great men who have lived in America and have helped to make and keep it great.

Today I feel as if an anchor, one whom I could reach out and touch when I needed friendly advice, a wonderful companion has left me, and he will not return. But in the years to come, however many may be allotted to me, I will cherish and memory will be green when I think of my old friend.

Added to his great capacity as a statesman he was also a gentleman of the first order, kindly, with no venom. His weapon was his argument and the way he could assemble and put his facts before the people. He was a great leader of men.

He was a great family man. I have known all of his children and practically all of his grandchildren. Both of his lovely helpmeets I knew, and they were friends of mine, because they knew I was a friend of the great man who

walked hand in hand with them. Few times in our lifetime—
it matters not how long it is—do we see his like. I may not
see his like again, but I know this today, that out there somewhere where the mighty spirits are gathered, the approach
of ALBEN BARKLEY was received with open arms, because he
was the equal of the mightest spirits that assemble wherever
that land or that clime may be. God bless his memory. God
comfort his loved ones—God comfort me.

Mr. SPENCE. Mr. Speaker, I yield to our distinguished
majority leader the gentleman from Massachusetts [Mr.
McCormack].

Mr. McCORMACK. Mr. Speaker, the country in the death
of Senator ALBEN BARKLEY has lost one of its greatest citizens
of all times. His life is an inspiration for all to follow and
a heritage that brings great consolation to his loved ones.
Kentucky today has a heavy heart as my friend the gentleman from Kentucky [Mr. Spence] well said. I agree with
him; I might add that the country has a heavy heart, for his
death leaves a gap that will take long to fill. ALBEN BARKLEY
and I were very close friends. There is no one I admired
more than I admired ALBEN BARKLEY.

During World War II, ALBEN BARKLEY and I served as majority leaders of our respective bodies. I can testify to his
greatness and his courage as evidenced by the meetings of
the leaders with the late Franklin D. Roosevelt, and of ALBEN
BARKLEY's wise advice on many occasion in the best interest
of our country. In the 1952 Democratic National Convention, I spoke and voted for the nomination of ALBEN BARKLEY
as the Democratic nominee for President. That will always
be one of the most satisfactory and happy occasions and
votes that I have ever made or will ever make. ALBEN
BARKLEY was a great Democrat. He firmly believed in the
two-party system as the most effective means for our people
to express their political views in the best interests of our
country. He believed in the unity and solidarity of the

Democratic Party which he loved with a great devotion and a lifetime of service. He abhorred disservice and disunity. He condemned the policy of some that either they rule or they ruin. No matter how trying the situation was ALBEN BARKLEY, a strong disciple of Thomas Jefferson, believed that party came first. But, over and above his strong party adherence, ALBEN BARKLEY stood for his country first. He always raised his voice and his influence within the Democratic Party so that the Democratic policy, whether a Democrat or a Republican President was in the White House, should strengthen the national interests of our country and always be for the best interests of our people.

In the years preceding World War II, ALBEN BARKLEY was a bulwark of strength in frustrating and later defeating Hitler and nazism. At the very moment of his death he was a bulwark of strength in the fight against atheistic communism. Throughout a lifetime of public service he was a great progressive, always in his vision of progressive measures trying to preserve and strengthen America and its family life.

One could go on endlessly talking about ALBEN BARKLEY. ALBEN BARKLEY's name in American history is established for all time. The name of ALBEN BARKLEY is now included among the great Americans of yesterday.

I extend to Mrs. Barkley and her loved ones my very deep sympathy in their great loss and sorrow. I also extend my sympathy to my colleagues from Kentucky.

Mr. SPENCE. Mr. Speaker, I yield to the gentleman from Virginia [Mr. Harrison].

Mr. HARRISON of Virginia. Mr. Speaker, it has fallen to my lot to have been the only Member of either the House or the Senate to have been with the Vice President on his last day on earth. As a matter of fact, since last Thursday he and I have conducted a sort of tour of my district. On Thursday he attended the Apple Blossom Festival in Winchester at which his granddaughter presided as queen. On

Sunday he was back again and spent the day with Senator
Byrd at a party at his home in Clarke County; and then
again on yesterday at the mock convention at Washington
and Lee University. During all that time I have never known
him to be in finer fettle or more himself. I suppose he told
a thousand stories and shook the hands of thousands of people. And he entered into the spirit of each occasion where
he was.

Washington and Lee University for nearly 50 years has
conducted these mock conventions. They hold regular conventions and they put a great deal into it. On yesterday
Senator BARKLEY and I drove through a 2-hour parade, and
from every window of the small town of Lexington loud-
speakers blasted the virtues of Adlai Stevenson, Estes Kefauver, and Governor Harriman. It was obvious that he was
enjoying himself immensely.

When he was introduced to the convention, in which every
State was represented by delegates, he was received with
great enthusiasm. The occasion called for him to make a
partisan Democratic speech, and he rose to the occasion
nobly. He made a ripsnortin', old-fashioned, rootin' tootin'
Democratic speech that delighted his audience. He began
with the early days of the Republic and came down to the
present day and held forth on the theme that every good
thing that was ever accomplished in the history of this country was due to the Democratic Party and every bad thing that
had ever befallen the country was due to the machinations
of the Republican Party. And I might add, Mr. Speaker, that
he almost proved it. And yet he did it in a way that had no
sting, or would give offense to anyone.

During the course of his talk he recited the number of
Democratic conventions he had attended—every one since
1920, and he said he had been thinking about not going to
this one, but because of the spirit of this occasion the old
firehorse felt that he could not stay away. He led up to
the words that have been quoted here by saying that in look-

ing at the floats—there were floats for Harriman, for Kefauver, and for Stevenson—that if he had not known before he came there he would have learned from the floats that he was not a candidate for President this year.

Someone called out: "What about the old firehorse?"

He replied, "All the old firehorses are gone; the departments now are run by motor vehicles."

A few minutes before the end, I felt that he was hurrying his speech to a conclusion.

Then he recited his career as a junior Member of the House, as a senior Member of the House, as a junior Senator and as a senior Senator, majority leader, Vice President, and now again a junior Senator.

Then he closed with the words that have been quoted.

He fell to the floor. He suffered no pain. He gasped a few times and he was gone.

I would like to say one more word, and that is that during her ordeal his charming and gallant widow conducted herself with a courage and a grace that he would have wanted and expected of her.

We went back to the home of the President of Washington and Lee University and there they were recording in the guest book that he had signed that day at lunch the exact verbiage of his closing words. She asked me if that was in accordance with my recollection: "I would rather be a servant in the house of the Lord than to sit in the seats of the mighty."

I said: "Now, Mrs. Barkley, he sits on the right hand of God."

She smiled through her tears and said: "No, not yet; I doubt if he has finished telling St. Peter his stories."

There is something very fitting about all this and the way he went. He was twitted during the day because he had graduated in law at a rival institution, the University of Virginia; and here this son of Lincoln's Kentucky in his closing speech defended his education at Jefferson's University of Virginia, and he fell and died at the university endowed by and named for George Washington, and his body was taken to rest in the home of Robert E. Lee.

I feel that he would have wanted all that.

Mr. WATTS. Mr. Speaker, the death of ALBEN BARKLEY comes as a profound shock to all of us. It seems that in His plan of things the Almighty has provided that each generation will have an outstanding leader in a particular chosen field—an individual endowed with talent so extraordinary that he stands above comparison. It seems that this individual is especially touched by the hands of the Creator to be the example and the goal toward which all who would succeed must steer their course. Such a man was ALBEN BARKLEY. But, Mr. Speaker, ALBEN BARKLEY was an exception to this exceptional rule. ALBEN BARKLEY excelled in statesmanship. He was possessed of an overabundance of those traits of character and human qualities from which flow the true spirit of Christianity and reflect the personification of gentlemanly principles.

ALBEN BARKLEY died while pronouncing the rule by which he lived. Measured by material wealth, his origin was laid deeply in the lower echelons. Measured by those intangibles of spiritual and character-building qualities, his origin was unsurpassed in its richness. He came from pioneer stock of the early Kentuckians. His boyhood and his early manhood were cloaked in an environment requiring long days of hard and arduous toil for mere survival. Throughout the whole of this, Mr. Speaker, the light of ALBEN BARKLEY's exceptional qualities shone with the brilliance of the sun. The pinnacle that he achieved was willed to him by the people whom he served and whom he loved in an effort to evidence their respect, their esteem, and their affection for him.

Mr. Speaker, this Nation has suffered a terrific loss. Because of his vast experience in Government, his firsthand knowledge of international and domestic problems, his impeccable character and his love of country, the Nation was afforded a guarantor of its security and a defender of its freedoms that will be difficult to replace.

Yes, Mr. Speaker, ALBEN BARKLEY was great, but he was humble. Truly, today he must be "a servant in the house of the Lord."

I join with a saddened and mournful Nation in extending heartfelt sympathy to the members of his family.

Mr. EVINS. Mr. Speaker, the good Lord in his infinite wisdom last evening called to his side one of the truly great leaders of our time. The loss of Senator ALBEN BARKLEY will be felt in this Nation and the Halls of our Congress for years to come.

His warm, human, and colorful personality and quick intellect gathered him a host of friends during his fruitful life and he will be greatly missed by all.

The New York Times of this morning contains an editorial in memory of the great Democratic leader from Kentucky and, under unanimous consent, I ask that this editorial be printed in the Record, together with my own brief but sincere remarks of admiration for this great American:

ALBEN W. BARKLEY

"I would rather be a servant in the house of the Lord than sit in the seats of the mighty" was the sentence ALBEN BARKLEY had just completed when death claimed him in the middle of an address he was delivering at Washington and Lee University. In his lifetime ALBEN BARKLEY had, indeed, sat in the seat of the mighty, but this United States Senator and former Vice President never lost the humility and common touch of a servant in the house of the Lord as he served the American people in their legislative halls.

History will remember ALBEN BARKLEY for his sponsorship of, and leadership in putting through, much of the important and beneficial social legislation of the thirties. It will remember him for his leadership in such grave matters as lend lease and ratification of the United Nations Charter. It will remember him for the high offices he has held, for the good work he has done in those high offices, and for the powerful influence he bore in getting opposing factions to compromise their differences in times of emergency.

But now we think of him for his warm, human, colorful qualities, for the respect and affection he evoked in others, not least of whom were the voters of Kentucky who elected him time and again to office. A vital man, he had much still to give his country, even at the age of 79. He will be sorely missed and long remembered.

Mr. ALBERT. Mr. Speaker, I take this means of imparting to the House an impression which I have always had of Senator BARKLEY. He was a man of tremendous accomplishments, but it is not of these that I speak. I admired him as I admired few men, not because he was the best storyteller I ever heard; not because he was campaign orator and stump speaker without a peer in this generation; not because he was elected Congressman, Senator, and Vice President; but because, through his life and ideals, he gave dignity and sublimity to the concept of public service. It is an honor to hold public office because ALBEN W. BARKLEY held public office.

Mr. EDMONDSON. Mr. Speaker, it is difficult to add anything of beauty or of substance to the eloquent tributes we have heard today to the memory of the great Kentuckian, Senator ALBEN W. BARKLEY.

In the hearts of Oklahomans, whom he had inspired and challenged on many speaking occasions, he was one of the real giants of this century—a peerless orator, a courageous statesman, and a man in every noble sense of the word.

In 1952, at the Democratic National Convention in Chicago, he received the votes of Oklahoma for nomination as our presidential candidate—and no higher tribute can be paid by a State.

I am proud of the fact that the Sooner State recognized and honored the greatness of ALBEN BARKLEY. The grief and sadness in the hearts of Senator BARKLEY's loved ones, and of Americans everywhere, are fully shared in Oklahoma.

Mr. PRIEST. Mr. Speaker, measured by all standards, Senator BARKLEY was truly a great man, a stalwart statesman, and a public servant wholly devoted to the welfare of the people of this country and to the cause of peace in the world.

There was in his last moment an element of quiet drama, sometimes found in fiction, but seldom in life.

We are saddened in this hour because ALBEN BARKLEY'S quality of friendship was of such character that it was cherished as a very personal thing by all who knew him.

Death has hushed a vibrant voice that embellished with brilliance the oratorical annals of our time.

But the lingering overtones of that voice and the presence of his personality shall be felt long after his body is laid to rest under a canopy of bluegrass in his old Kentucky home.

To his widow and his family I extend my sincerest sympathy.

Mr. REED of New York. Mr. Speaker, the sudden passing of Hon. ALBEN W. BARKLEY, United States Senator from Kentucky, came as a great personal shock to me. He is a man whom I have known ever since I have been a Member of Congress and for whom I have always entertained the highest esteem and affection. I regard Senator BARKLEY as one of the outstanding statesmen of all time and a man who had few if any enemies.

It was only a short time ago that I appointed him to undertake a most important mission in Dubrovnik, Yugoslavia, to meet with the Council of the Interparliamentary Union. Associated with him was Senator A. Willis Robertson, of Virginia. Both of these distinguished men undertook this trip as a patriotic duty and used their Easter vacation to perform a herculean task in the field of statesmanship. They were successful on their mission, which was to keep Red China from becoming a member of the Interparliamentary Union until such time as it should become recognized by the United Nations. Both Senators had to meet with terrific pressure from Communist countries, but I repeat they were successful.

I am deeply disturbed that this long trip which Senator BARKLEY was perfectly willing and anxious to make may have pressed heavily on his limited strength.

I want to say in conclusion that his passing is a source of great grief to all who knew him and my sympathy goes out to his wife and family in this terrible bereavement.

Mr. BURDICK. Mr. Speaker, a giant tree in the forest has fallen. The winds and storms of 50 years of public service, with extra burdens demanded by the people, loosed the roots of this great tree and it fell among its fellows, leaving a vast void where it once stood.

ALBEN BARKLEY was endowed by nature with extraordinary gifts. He could reduce complicated questions to such simple terms that all men who were fortunate enough to hear him could understand. Opponents on legislative and legal questions took no offense at his position and applauded the manner in which he maintained his case.

Though one of the most sincere and earnest men in public life for half a century, he did not fail to see humorous things. His powers of ridicule and invective were devastating, and storied applications in his arguments were powerful and convincing. As an advocate of public and legal questions he had, in this era, no superior, and in defending questions which he conceived to be for the best interests of the people he was a master.

While circumstances prevented him from becoming President of the United States, he was bigger than Presidents in the times in which he lived.

His last earthly utterance, "I would rather be a servant in the house of the Lord than sit in the seats of the mighty" summed up his life. This utterance will be a motto for human conduct long after the present generation shall have passed into the shadows of the Great Unknown, and for as long as the principles of this great Republic shall endure.

One of the truly great men of our generation has made his last speech and in it has left for all future generations a perfect definition of a public servant.

Mr. MACK of Illinois. Mr. Speaker, yesterday this Nation lost a great and courageous statesman with the death of ALBEN W. BARKLEY, of Kentucky.

His splendid record of more than 50 years of public service stands as a monument to his unselfish dedication of his life to the welfare of his fellow man and to his country.

His loss will be keenly felt by all of us, and memories of his valued service will stand as a challenge to all who are dedicated to public service.

Mr. GRAY. Mr. Speaker, will the gentleman yield?

Mr. SPENCE. I yield.

Mr. GRAY. Mr. Speaker, I rise today with a sorrowing heart to join with all my colleagues, the beloved Speaker, and the people of the entire United States in mourning the passing of ALBEN W. BARKLEY. I was born and raised just a few miles across the Ohio River from Paducah, Ky., and since a small child I have learned to love, respect, and admire ALBEN BARKLEY. He was a very personal friend of mine. He was a guiding hand to me.

As I stand here today I think of those words "Greater love hath no man than this, than he who is willing to lay down his life for his friends."

ALBEN BARKLEY was that type of man. It made no difference when you went to him, day or night, he was always willing to help you and to give you a little advice or to come into your district or to assist you in any manner he possibly could.

I may say that his home at Paducah is separated from my district only by the width of the Ohio River. My people in southern Illinois join me with bowed heads and sorrowing hearts at the passing of this great American.

At this time I think of those words once again:

Man that is born of a woman is of a few days, and full of trouble.

He cometh forth like a flower, and is cut down; he fleeth also as a shadow, and continueth not.

So we must all expect the inevitable, but we are never willing to give up such good friends, such great statesmen as was ALBEN BARKLEY.

In closing, I want to join with all of my colleagues and all Americans in extending the most sincere sympathy to Mrs. Barkley and the other members of the family. I know that words we utter here today will not ease the grief that is theirs, but I would like to say that this country is greater, its people are greater, because ALBEN W. BARKLEY passed this way. God bless all of us in this hour of sorrow.

Mr. COOLEY. Mr. Speaker, will the gentleman yield?

Mr. SPENCE. I yield to the gentleman from North Carolina.

Mr. COOLEY. Mr. Speaker, for many years I have enjoyed the friendship of the great man whose memory we at this moment honor. I have been very closely associated with our beloved colleague and I have known him intimately and well; I have admired and loved him through the years.

ALBEN W. BARKLEY was a citizen of the world, and today the liberty-loving people of the universe are mourning his death. This great man was not only loved in Kentucky; he was not only loved in America; but he was loved and admired by the men of many races in all parts of the world.

Because of our mutual interest in the welfare of the tobacco farmers of our Nation and of our mutual interest and activities in the Interparliamentary Union, we have been very closely associated with each other. Mr. BARKLEY, as chairman of the American group of the Interparliamentary Union, designated me as a delegate to the first meeting of that great organization, which I attended approximately 10 years ago. It was because of his great interest in the activities and the affairs of that organization that I became interested and finally was elected as a member of the nine-man executive committee of the Interparliamentary Union, in which the lawmakers of 46 nations of the world are now participating.

I recall with pleasant memories our visit together to the Holy Land, the place where Christ was born, en route to Cairo for the first postwar meeting of the Union. Our distinguished colleague was loved and respected and held in high esteem by members of that great organization which has labored through the years for peace and a better world understanding. He is the only member of the American Senate to my knowledge who has served on the executive committee of the Interparliamentary Union. When I was elected to the executive committee, I, of course, deemed it a great honor. During the Easter holidays the executive committee met in Dubrovnik, Yugoslavia. It was an important meeting; but as chairman of the House Committee on Agriculture, it was necessary for me to remain in Washington and to forego this meeting in Yugoslavia because the farm bill was in conference. I knew that Red China was seeking admission to the Interparliamentary Union and that the petitions of Red China would have the support of Russia and all of its satellites. The State Department had urged me to attend this meeting, but I considered the farm problems of America of paramount importance and could not abandon my post of duty here.

In this situation I turned to my beloved friend, the distinguished statesman of the world, ALBEN W. BARKLEY. I discussed the matter with him in the Democratic cloakroom in the Senate, and he agreed with me that under no circumstances should I leave Washington because of the importance of the farm bill. I then asked him if he would go as my alternate and substitute to attend this very important meeting. Mr. BARKLEY said, "I will talk it over with Mrs. Barkley; and if I can possibly do so, I will."

He finally advised me that he would represent me at the meeting of the executive committee in Yugoslavia. I went to the airport to see them off and to bid them bon voyage. On that day the Barkleys were happy and lighthearted as we waved to them on their last voyage together across the sea.

Mr. BARKLEY was successful in his efforts at the meeting at Dubrovnik.

This great man, whom we honor at this moment, could not have died more gloriously nor could he have lived more magnificently. When I think of his political life and the political campaigns in which he has engaged, I know that he was always guided and directed by the impulses and sentiments expressed in these brief words:

When the one great Scorer comes to write against my name,
He will write not that I won or lost but how I played the game.

I also think of a poem:

Oh, heart of mine, we should worry so
What we've missed of calm we couldn't have, you know!
What we've met of stormy pain and of sorrow's driving rain
We can better meet again if it blow!
For we know not every morrow can be sad;
So forget all the sorrow we have had.
Let us fold away our fears and put by our foolish tears,
And through all the coming years just be glad.

I am glad that I knew ALBEN W. BARKLEY. May we through all the coming years just be glad that we have known and loved this great man and have worked and labored with him here in the Halls of Congress.

We need not build a monument to the memory of ALBEN W. BARKLEY. He has built for himself many magnificent and beautiful monuments in the hearts of his friends throughout the world. His life was a blessing and a benediction to all mankind.

Mr. Speaker, I extend to his lovely and devoted wife and to all the members of his family my very deep and profound sympathy.   May God bless them all.

Mrs. ROGERS of Massachusetts.   Mr. Speaker, yesterday the United States of America, and the world received a crushing blow.   When the porter on my train called me this morning he said, "Mrs. Rogers, don't you think we have lost a wonderfully fine man and a great Senator?   He was never bitter."   We have lost more than words can convey in the death of ALBEN BARKLEY, one of the greatest Americans we have ever known, one of the greatest Christians we have ever known, and one of the greatest friends we have ever had.

Mr. Speaker, I mourn with you and all the Members his passing, and I mourn with his gallant and beautiful wife that he loved dearly and his family that he loved so much, and I mourn with his beautiful State of Kentucky.

Mr. BOGGS.   Mr. Speaker, in the market place of public affairs good men and great men have influence far beyond their own knowledge.   Most of the time they themselves are unaware of their own impact.   Such a man died on Monday last, ALBEN W. BARKLEY.

I saw a great deal of Senator BARKLEY in the last 10 days of his life.   For him I am certain that they were happy days as, I believe, were most of his days.   Beginning on Saturday, April 21, I saw him and listened to him at the Democratic testimonial dinner for Woodrow Wilson.   There he delivered, in his usual magnificent style, a moving tribute to a great American who had undoubtedly greatly influenced ALBEN W. BARKLEY himself.

On the following Monday I went to a luncheon in the Senate where he gave a report on the approaching meeting of the Interparliamentary Union in Bangkok, Thailand.   I marvelled at his knowledge of world affairs, his approach to the problems of other peoples and other government, and his sustaining interest in public affairs.

And then on Wednesday night of last week at the annual Press Club party for the Members of Congress he stole the show—his wit, his humor, his humility, his understanding brought him a standing ovation from members of the press and from his colleagues of both parties in both branches of the Congress.

On Saturday last, April 28, the National Broadcasting Co. was celebrating the 10th anniversary of its famous program, Meet the Press. The principal speaker was Senator BARKLEY. His attendance at that program was his last public appearance in the Capitol of the country that he loved and served so well. On that night he spoke of our basic freedoms of press and our right to information. He emphasized the importance of an informed electorate in a democracy. He told how the dictators, either of the left or of the right, invariably suppress information. And on that night he did something that I had seldom heard him do—he reminisced. Normally he looked to the future in discussing the problems of the present. But he talked about his years in Congress dating back to 1913—years of service which covered the rise to greatness of the United States of America.

And on Monday, fully in character, talking to young Americans he died saying, "I would rather be a servant in the house of the Lord than sit in the seat of the mighty." He wrote his own magnificent epitaph.

Mr. Speaker, this man shall live in the hearts of all Americans. His life portrayed the man—his sincerity of purpose, his humility—his love of party, his paramount love of country.

I believe those of us who serve in public office appreciate more than others sincerity of purpose. Unfortunately there are some who come to public office who, in pursuit of the sensational, the headlines, and the acclaim of the moment, sacrifice sincerity and objectivity. Their colleagues get to know them and they cease to have any influence.

Yes, Mr. Speaker, Senator BARKLEY was the epitome of the American ideal of public service. He understood the greatness of America and the goodness of America, and because of him our country is stronger and better and happier.

Mr. ROONEY. Mr. Speaker, I was profoundly shocked this morning when I heard of the tragic passing of Senator ALBEN W. BARKLEY, of Kentucky.

He was one of the finest men I ever knew, and I am sure that his place in the hearts of many of us will never be filled. When he suddenly fell near the end of a speech at Washington and Lee University's mock Democratic Convention, he apparently died almost instantly. It is fitting to note that his passing occurred in an atmosphere he loved best—the political forum. He always enjoyed and liked young people, and he was idolized and deeply admired by them as they saw in him the personification of those qualities we have always sought in our national leaders.

In September of 1948 it was my great privilege to accompany Senator BARKLEY to Europe to attend an Interparliamentary Union Conference in Rome. We visited Madrid, Paris, and Berlin, and I can well recall the trip as one of the highlights of my life.

The Senator was a man whose courtly manners and gallantry added much to the happiness and public life of our country. He was a real southern gentleman, and his penetrating intellect, wit, and wisdom endeared him in the hearts of the American people. His passing is not only a great loss to the Nation but also to the entire civilized world. His distinguished career as a Congressman, Senator, and a great Vice President has never been surpassed.

I join with my colleagues in mourning this lovable and outstanding public servant and extend to his widow, children, and grandchildren, my deepest sympathy in their hour of bereavement.

Mr. ZABLOCKI. Mr. Speaker, the news of the sudden passing away of Senator ALBEN BARKLEY brought deep and sincere sorrow not only to his colleagues, and to the people of the State of Kentucky, but to our entire Nation.

In the turbulent decades of our recent history, the name of ALBEN BARKLEY became known in every household across the land. ALBEN BARKLEY—whose entire life was devoted to public service—became the personification of the wise and benevolent statesman that boys dream of becoming, and that men strive to emulate. His dedication to the public interest; his gracious manner; and his inimitable art of story telling endeared him to the hearts of the American people.

In the death of our beloved Veep, we have lost more than a distinguished public servant. We have lost a part of Americana that may never be duplicated again. We have lost a man, a leader who came from the best tradition of the past but who looked to the future and who strove with all the energy at his disposal to fashion a better Nation and a better world for all of us to enjoy.

We are aggrieved by his death, but proud that we have lived in the same age with him and known him. His name shall go down in history for he has served his country well.

I wish to extend my deepest sympathy to his widow and his family in their bereavement. May they be consoled in their loss in the thought that the good Lord has chosen him to be among His very own.

Mr. SPENCE. Mr. Speaker, I offer a resolution (H. Res. 491) and ask for its immediate consideration.

The Clerk read the resolution, as follows:

Resolved, That the House has heard with profound sorrow of the death of Hon. ALBEN W. BARKLEY, a Senator of the United States from of the State of Kentucky; formerly Vice President of the United States and a former Member of the House of Representatives from the State of Kentucky.

Resolved, That the Clerk communicate these resolutions and transmit a copy thereof to the family of the deceased Senator.

Resolved, That a committee of eight Members be appointed on the part of the House to join the committee appointed on the part of the Senate to attend the funeral.

The resolution was agreed to.

The **SPEAKER**. The Chair appoints as members of the funeral committee the following members on the part of the House: Mr. Spence, Mr. Gregory, Mr. Chelf, Mr. Perkins, Mr. Watts, Mr. Robsion, Mr. Natcher, Mr. Siler.

The Clerk will report the remainder of the resolution.

The Clerk read as follows:

Resolved, That as a further mark of respect to the memory of the deceased the House do now adjourn.

The resolution was agreed to.

Accordingly (at 12 o'clock and 58 minutes p. m.) the House adjourned until tomorrow, Wednesday, May 2, 1956, at 12 o'clock noon.

THURSDAY, *May 3, 1956.*

A message from the Senate, from Mr. McBride, one of its clerks, announced that the Senate had adopted the following resolution (S. Res. 258):

Resolved, That the Senate has heard with profound sorrow and deep regret the announcement of the death of Hon. ALBEN W. BARKLEY, late a Senator from the State of Kentucky and a former Vice President of the United States.

Resolved, That a committee be appointed by the President of the Senate, who shall be a member of the committee, to attend the funeral of the deceased Senator at Paducah, Ky.

Resolved, That the Secretary communicate these resolutions to the House of Representatives and transmit a copy thereof to the family of the deceased.

Resolved, That, as a further mark of respect to the memory of the deceased, the Senate do now adjourn.

Mr. PHILBIN. Mr. Speaker, to me, as to the American people, news of ALBEN BARKLEY's passing came as a great shock and brought a sense of deep, poignant grief. Only last Wednesday night, I attended a Congressional Night dinner and program at the National Press Club where this great man was an honored guest.

I had the opportunity again to meet and talk with him. He appeared to be his usual self. He was, as customary with him, genial, cordial, and good-humored. He addressed the gathering in the role of station announcer on the mock radio program being conducted by the famous television personality, Hal March, entitled "The Sixty-Four Billion Dollar Question."

As usual the great, noble son of Kentucky stole the show. With devastating shafts of humor and satire, he lampooned his political opponents while carrying out his assignment as station announcer. He seemed to be in good physical condition, was vigorous of manner and spirit, and he completely captivated the audience. It was the last time I was to see and hear ALBEN BARKLEY. A few days later I learned the sorrowful news of his most lamentable demise.

I had personally known ALBEN BARKLEY for many years. I had met him through my great, beloved friend, the late, distinguished Senator David I. Walsh, of Massachusetts, of revered and lamented memory. I had supported Senator BARKLEY at various Democratic Conventions for President and Vice President of the United States.

ALBEN BARKLEY was one of the outstanding statesmen of American history. I cannot here do justice to his life, his fine qualities, his superb abilities, his splendid achievements. That task is for others. But I desire to express my personal grief and extend my sympathy to his gracious helpmate and bereaved family.

He was a man of tremendous stature endowed by the Almighty with widely diverse talents and gifts. Of lovable personal traits, ready wit, good fellowship, interested in people, he had a remarkable sense of humor. He was a most engaging raconteur on and off the platform.

And he had a very deep religious and spiritual side to his nature which was manifest in his attitude throughout his life and was emphasized in an immemorable manner in the last words he spoke:

I would rather be a servant in the house of the Lord than sit in the seats of the mighty.

ALBEN BARKLEY made many eloquent speeches that will go down in history. But none will be so famous, so well-known, so much a part of future American life as that moving last sentence of his final speech.

He was a man of great strength, of power, of great gifts, and high position. He achieved great lasting distinction in political history and statescraft. But he kept his humble faith in the Lord to the very last breath of his honored being.

ALBEN BARKLEY will be long remembered with fond appreciation and utmost respect. For he was a sterling statesman in the best sense of the word, a truly great human being, an illustrious American.

Lawyer, jurist, Congressman, United States Senator, Vice President of the United States, he sat in truth in the seats of the mighty, but he always kept his faith in God, in his country, and his fellow man. And that will be his glorious, enduring epitaph.

THURSDAY, *May 17, 1956.*

Mr. BASS of Tennessee. Mr. Speaker, I ask unanimous consent to take from the Speaker's table the joint resolution (S. J. Res. 166) to designate the dam and reservoir to be constructed on the lower Cumberland River, Ky., as Barkley Dam and Lake Barkley, respectively, and ask for its immediate consideration.

The SPEAKER. Is there objection to the request of the gentleman from Tennessee?

There was no objection.

The Clerk read the Senate joint resolution, as follows:

Whereas the Congress is keenly aware that the late Senator ALBEN WILLIAM BARKLEY was so devoted to the people of the United States that he dedicated his life in unselfish public service to secure peace, to provide happiness, and to preserve freedom for the citizens of the United States, rising to the positions of Representative, Senator, and Vice President in said service; and

Whereas the Congress deems it fitting that the fine qualities of statesmanship, patriotism, and loyalty exemplified in the life of the late ALBEN WILLIAM BARKLEY should not be forgotten by the people he served so well: Now, therefore, be it

Resolved, etc., That the dam to be constructed on the lower Cumberland River, Ky., authorized by the Flood Control Act of 1954, and the reservoir to be formed by the waters impounded by such dam, shall hereafter be known as Barkley Dam and Lake Barkley, respectively, and any law, regulation, document, or record of the United States in which such dam and reservoir are designated or referred to shall be held to refer to such dam and reservoir under and by the name Barkley Dam and Lake Barkley, respectively.

The resolution was ordered to be read a third time, was read the third time, and passed, and a motion to reconsider was laid on the table.

Mr. BASS of Tennessee. Mr. Speaker, I introduced a resolution similar to Senate Joint Resolution 166, which was introduced by Senator Clements, of Kentucky, and passed by the Senate on yesterday. Since Senator Clements represents the State of our late and distinguished friend, Senator BARKLEY, I am more than happy to ask that his resolution be considered in lieu of the one that I introduced for the same purpose. I am very happy that the Congress through this means is able to pay tribute to an outstanding statesman, Senator, and Vice President, the late Hon. ALBEN W. BARKLEY, of Kentucky.

Memorial Tributes
to
Alben William Barkley

Memorial Tributes

❧

Remarks by Representative Wickersham
Of Oklahoma

Mr. WICKERSHAM.   Mr. Speaker, under leave to extend my remarks in the Record, I include the following editorials from the Evening Star and the Washington Post:

[From the Washington Star of May 1, 1956]

ALBEN BARKLEY

The American political stage has lost one of its favorite players in the death of ALBEN BARKLEY.   And that his death should come literally on stage while speaking lines that singularly reflected his innate humility, provided a fitting curtain for a memorable career.

ALBEN BARKLEY began life on a Kentucky farm.   When that life ended nearly 79 years later, it had become a mirror of three-quarters of a century of American history—the period in which a young but virile Nation arose from its post-Civil War suffering to move steadily on to unprecedented heights of greatness in strength and morality.   For most of that time, ALBEN BARKLEY played a major role.   Since 1913, save for the brief interlude of 1953–54, Mr. BARKLEY had been in the American Congress—eloquent as a youthful Congressman, powerful and persuasive as Senate majority leader during most of the New Deal period, benevolently forceful as Vice President.   As a junior Senator during the past 2 years, he was an elder statesman whose proud devotion to party was exceeded only by his devotion to country.

The years had dealt kindly to ALBEN BARKLEY and it was understandable to those who knew him.   Politics did not shape his character, or make of him a man obsessed with ambition and preoccupied with self-interest.   To a greater degree, it was the warmly human Kentuckian who left his impact on the politics of his time. His humor and his kindliness rubbed off on many of those who shared a place with him on the political stage.   It was fully in character that he died saying, "I would rather be a servant in the House of the Lord than sit in the seat of the mighty."

[159]

MEMORIAL ADDRESSES

[From the Washington Post and Times Herald of May 2, 1956]

ALBEN W. BARKLEY

Even in their expression of sorrow over the death of Senator ALBEN W. BARKLEY, his friends and acquaintances throughout the land are retelling his jokes, quips, and humorous stories. The big, good-natured man with the booming baritone voice made an impression on his fellow countrymen that will not soon be forgotten. Though he was a prodigious worker and a devoted public servant, he was never solemn about it. His hearty laugh and his spontaneous humor became his badge of identification and will ever be associated with his memory.

Mr. BARKLEY was a key figure in the history of the last two decades. People came to associate his name with almost every big contest which the Democratic Party waged in that period. Probably more than any living member of his party he was entitled to the cognomen of Mr. Democrat. But his partisanship had a genial quality that won him the affection of Republicans and Democrats alike. By relying upon humor instead of venom, he made his appeal universal.

His greatest work was done as majority leader in the Senate from 1937 to 1947. In that period he piloted through the Senate important legislation of Franklin D. Roosevelt's New Deal and Harry Truman's Fair Deal. Senator BARKLEY could be relied upon to go down the line for almost every administration measure. His record for party regularity in the House and later in the Senate was a large factor in his election as majority leader. The death of Senator Joseph T. Robinson in the midst of F. D. R.'s fight to enlarge the Supreme Court had left the Senate in a state of confusion. Only the President's intervention shifted the leadership to Mr. BARKLEY in preference to the more independent-minded Pat Harrison.

In appreciation for that support, Majority Leader BARKLEY stood by F. D. R. with remarkable tenacity through the prewar and war years. He was not, however, a man to be walked on. When Mr. Roosevelt wounded his sensibilities in a tax veto message, he resigned his leadership and was overwhelmingly reelected. This dramatic demonstration of confidence in him did not go to his head, nor did the incident turn him against F. D. R. A few months later he presented Mr. Roosevelt's name for a fourth presidential nomination.

Mr. BARKLEY would have been the logical choice for the vice presidential nomination in 1940 and 1944 if he could have been spared from the position of majority leader. His election to the

ALBEN WILLIAM BARKLEY

Vice Presidency in 1948 at the age of 71 was generally regarded as a reward for a lifetime of public service. But the Veep made it a working position and lent powerful support to the Truman administration without any show of sourness because a man of lesser political experience was in the White House. When Mr. BARKLEY, having retired from the Vice Presidency, once more demonstrated his vigor and invincibility in Kentucky by winning election to the Senate in 1954, he received an ovation from his former colleagues without any regard for party lines.

His friends and admirers were especially pleased when sunshine came to predominate in his personal life after long years of sorrow and struggle. His first wife, to whom he was devoted, Dorothy Brower, of Paducah, became an invalid, and he followed a rigorous schedule of lecturing, while he was majority leader, to pay the doctor bills her illness entailed. Mrs. Barkley died in 1947. Two years later, however, the hearty and irrepressible Veep met and married a charming widow, Mrs. Carleton S. Hadley, and this romance filled his remaining years with the warmth and satisfaction he had richly earned. ALBEN BARKLEY will be remembered as a man of many estimable human qualities, as well as a superb storyteller and a beloved leader in the great affairs of his day.

Remarks by Representative McDowell
Of Delaware

Mr. McDOWELL. Mr. Speaker, under leave to extend my remarks I would like to include the following resolutions adopted April 30, 1956, at the regular meeting of the Democratic League of Delaware:

MEMORIAL

At the regular meeting of the Democratic League of Delaware held Monday, April 30, 1956, the following resolutions were unanimously adopted:

"*Resolved,* That as members of the Democratic League of Delaware we record this expression of our sorrow at the death on Monday, April 30, 1956, of our fellow member, ALBEN W. BARKLEY.

"His long and unselfish service both to the Government of the United States and to the Democratic Party made him known, respected, and loved by all who hold dear the finest traditions of our American way of life. His vigorous and tireless efforts to further these traditions will ever live as one of the outstanding glories of the democratic ideal. Though we have lost his sparkling companionship and though his eloquent voice is now forever stilled, yet shall his memory live in our hearts as the symbol of the best of American initiative, political courage, and moral force.

"*Resolved,* That we extend to his family our most heartfelt sympathy in their bereavement, and that a copy of this memorial resolution be sent to them."

For the Democratic League of Delaware:

JOHN J. CLARKE, *President.*
JOHN A. HULL,
W. R. STEWART, Sr.,
HARRIS O. BUNEL,
FRANK T. DICKERSON, *Secretary.*